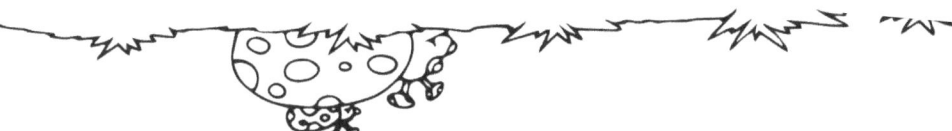

# Color Me Happy

Art.Z i
Art.Z illustrations
Griswold Ct
ArtZillustrations.com

Created and Printed in the USA

Illustrations by Bonnie S. MacLachlan

ISBN-13: 978-1947911871 (Art.Z illustrations)
ISBN-10: 1947911872

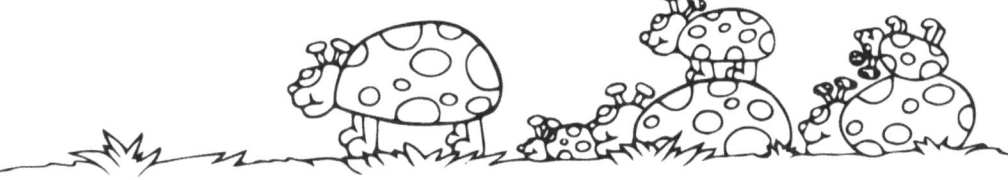

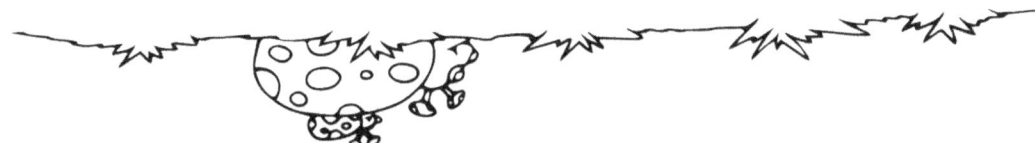

Art. Z illustrations
&
Bonnie S. MacLachlan
Introduce You To ...

# Color Me HaPpY
Adult Coloring Book

There are hidden little Lady Bugs through-out the book
Inspired By Bonnie's Love Of Lady Bugs   ;-)

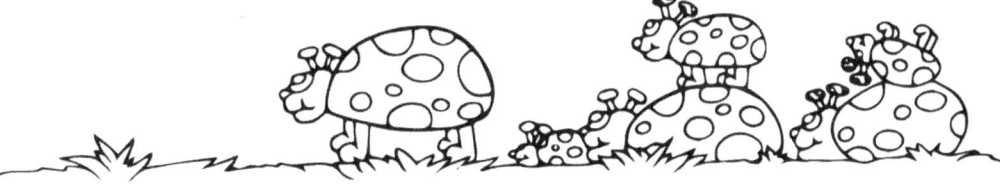

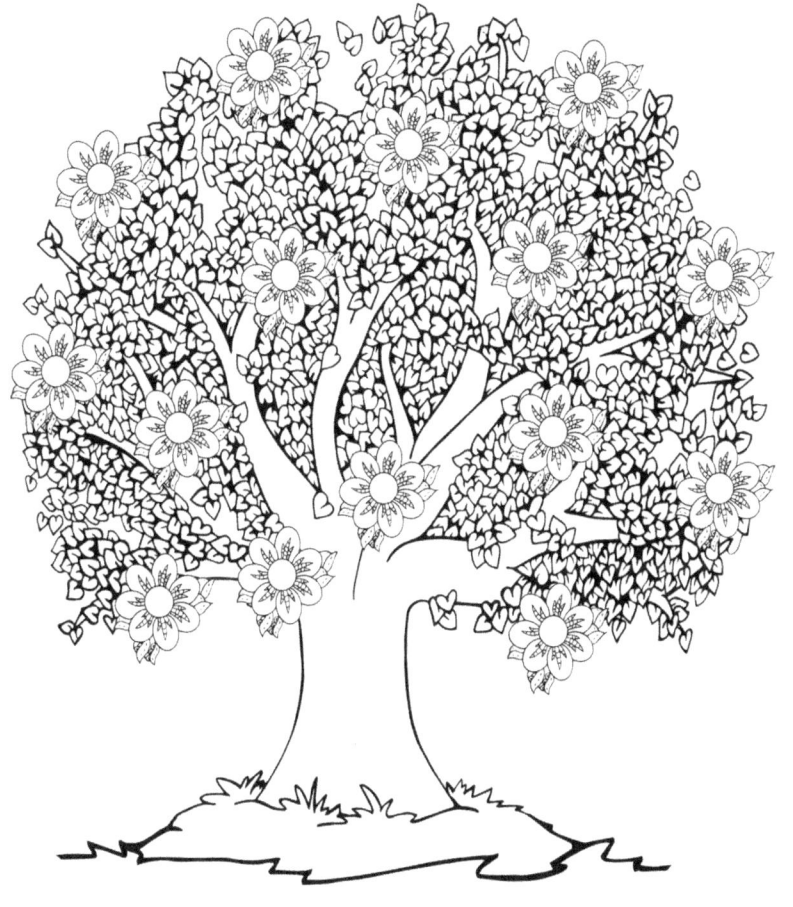

This Book Belongs To _____

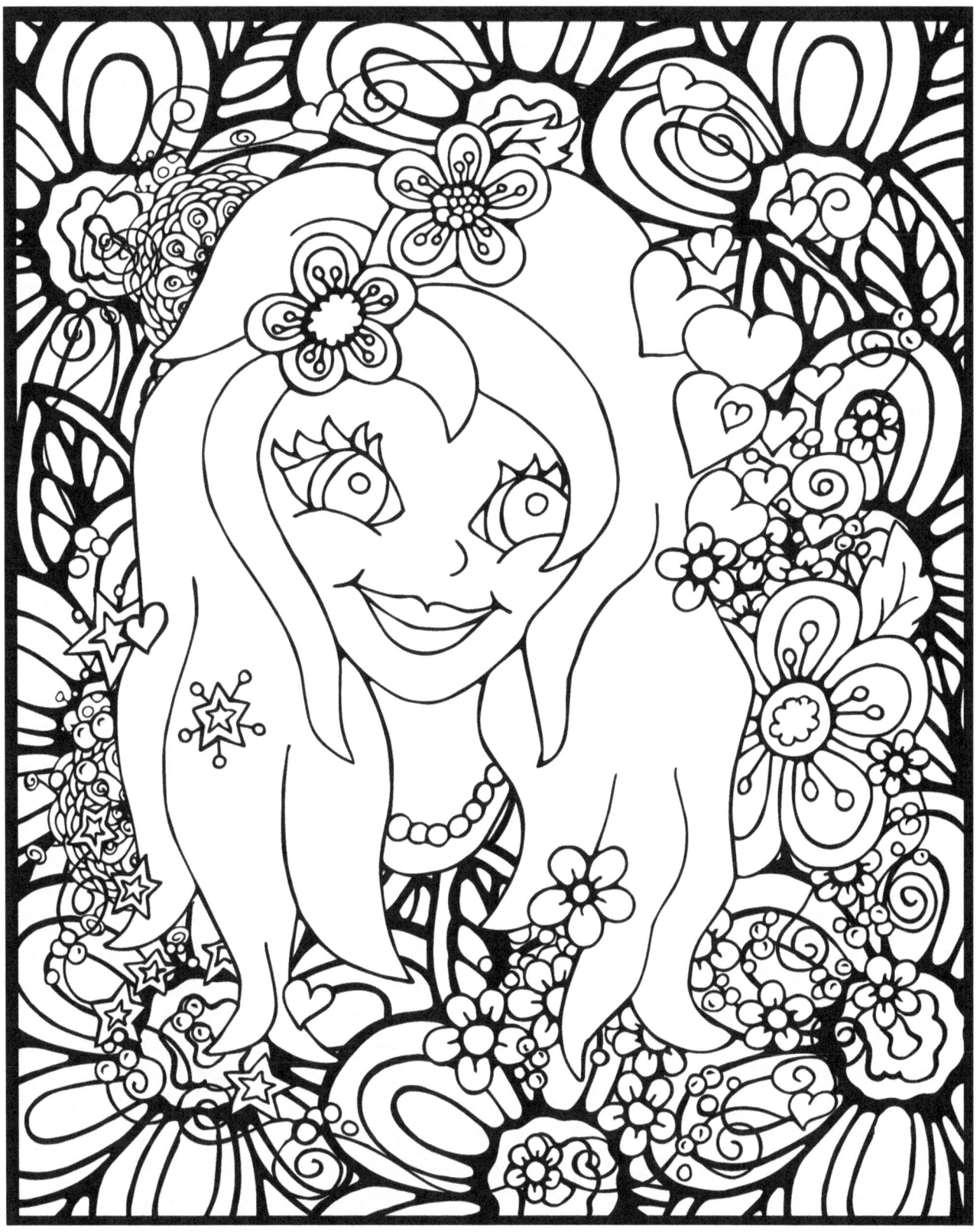

Bonnie S. MacLachlan                                                      Color Me HaPpY

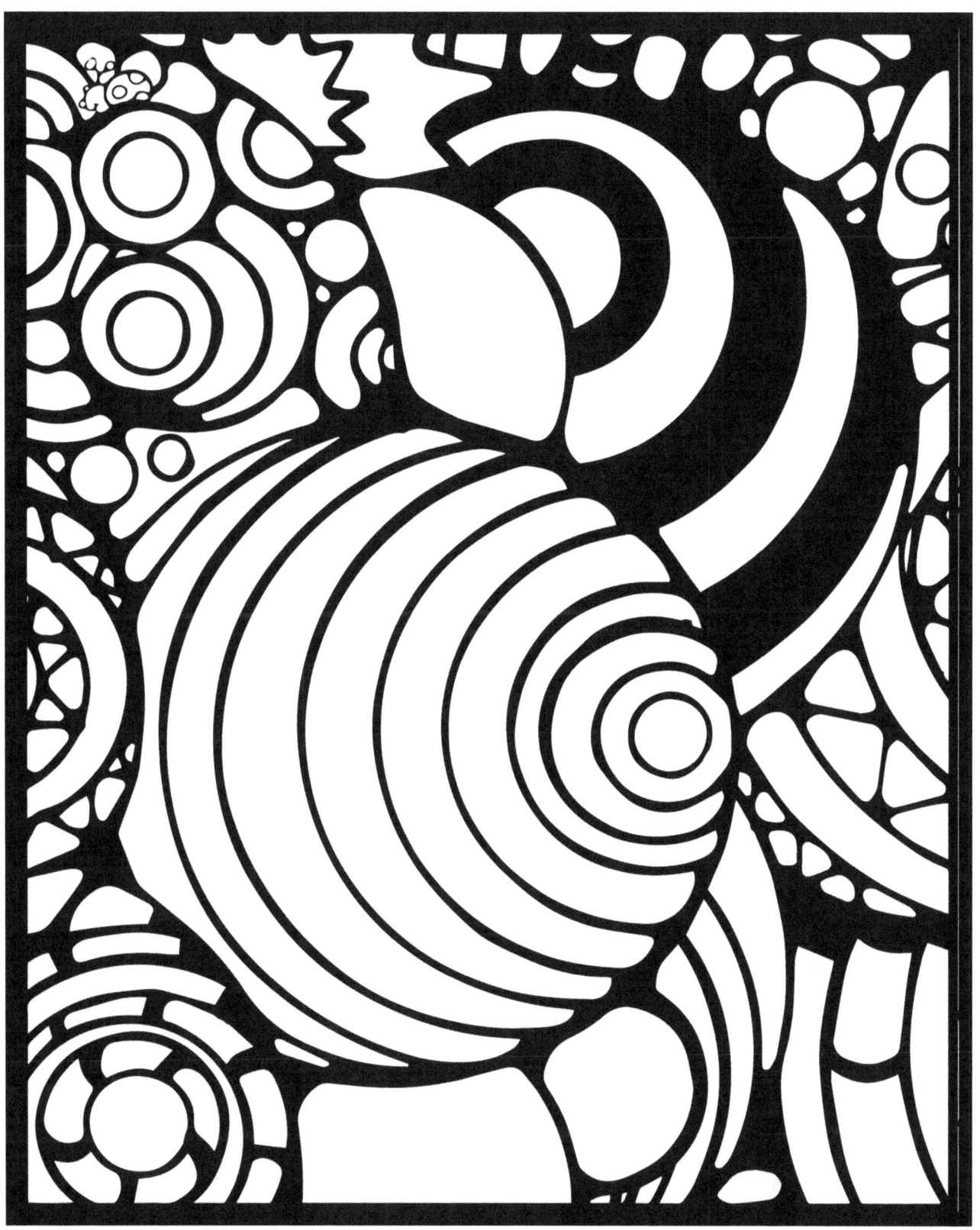

Bonnie S. MacLachlan

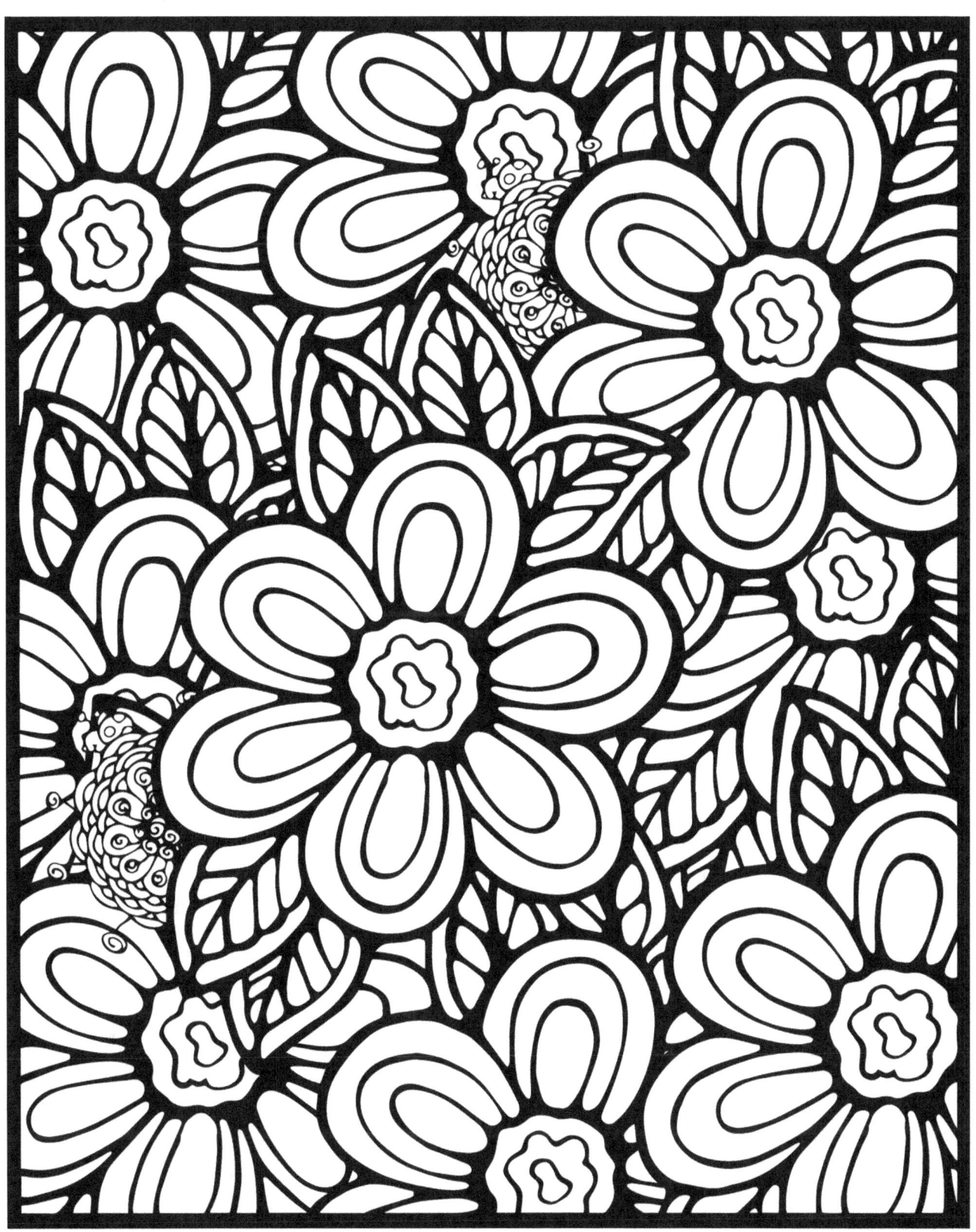

Bonnie S. MacLachlan

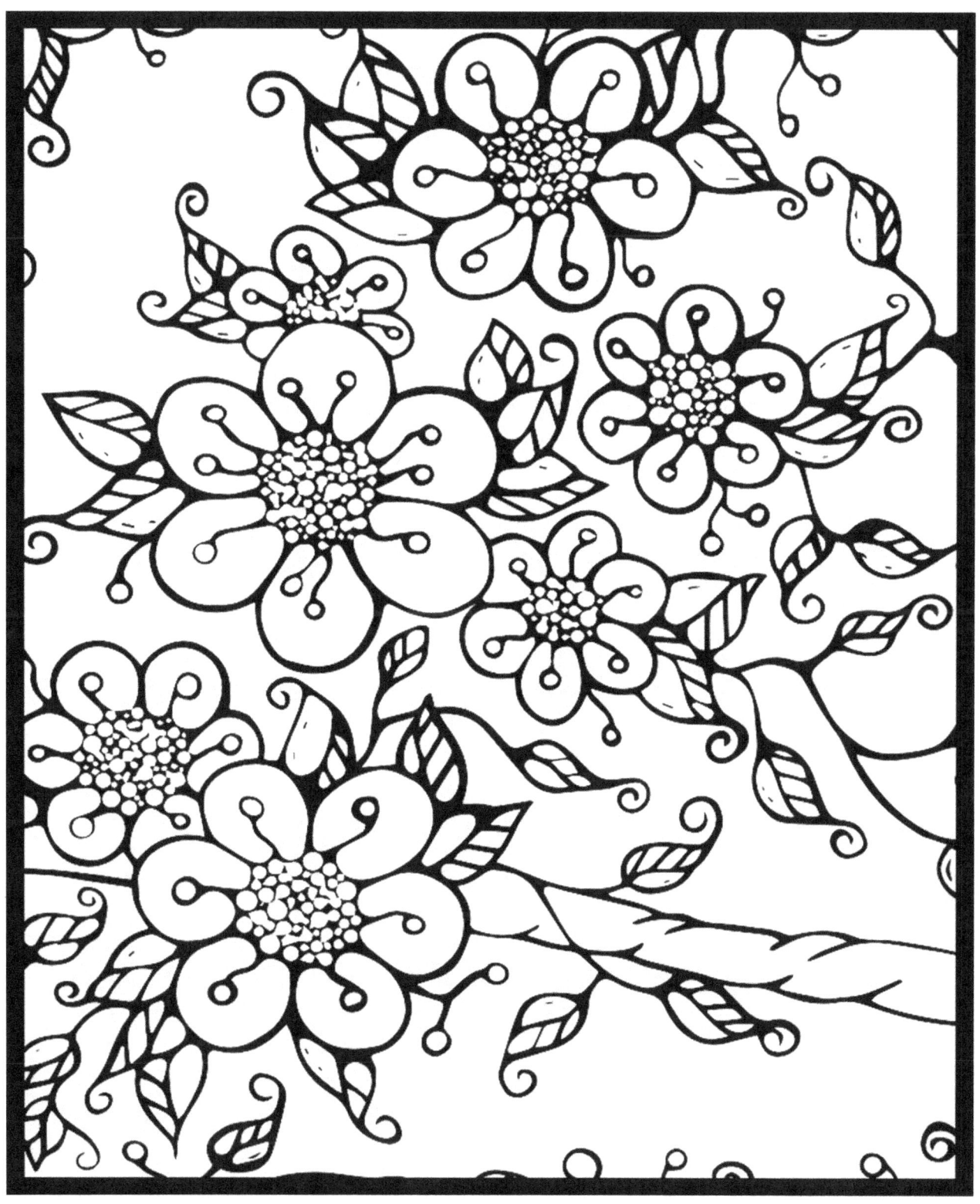

Bonnie S. MacLachlan

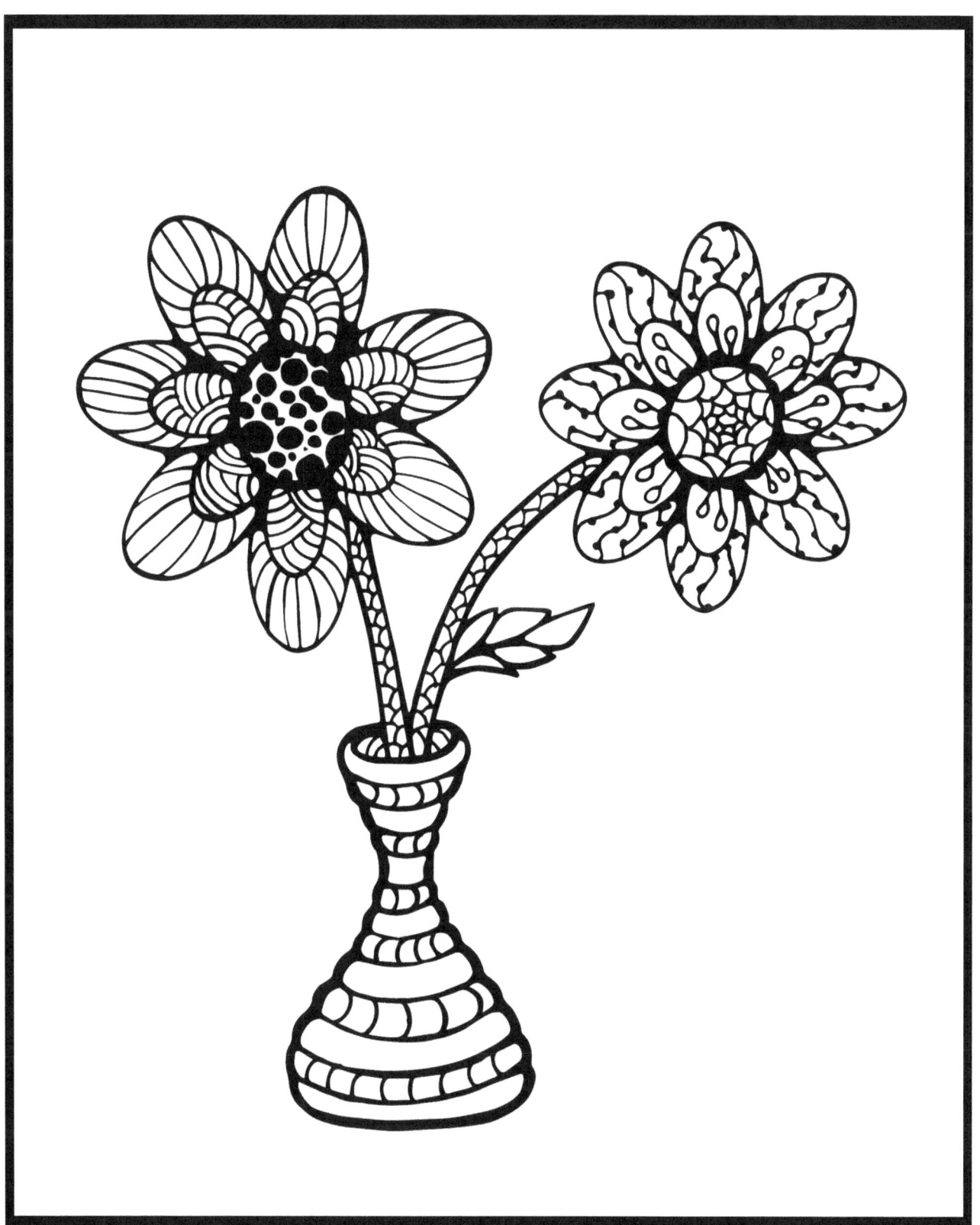

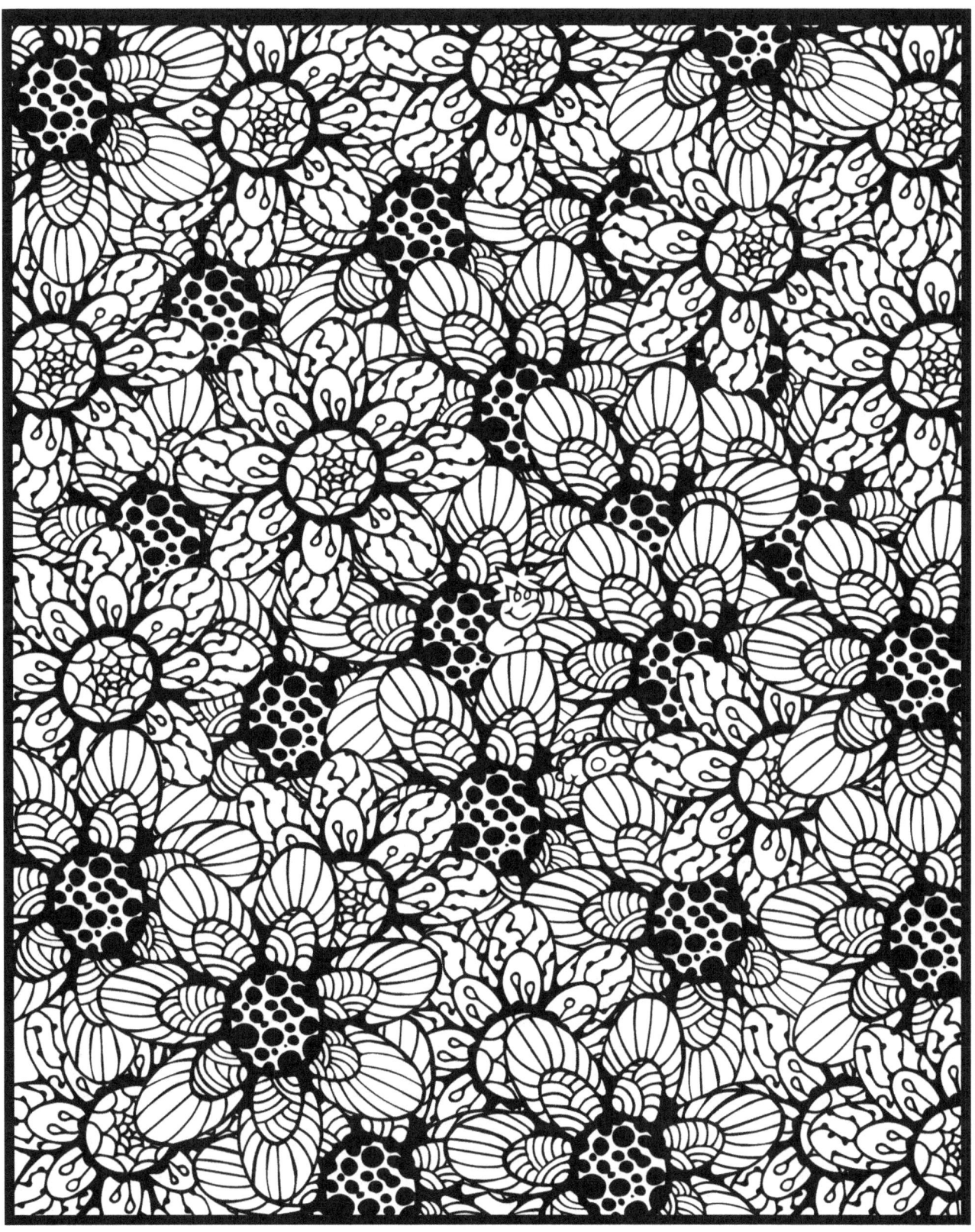

Bonnie S. MacLachlan

Color Me HaPpY

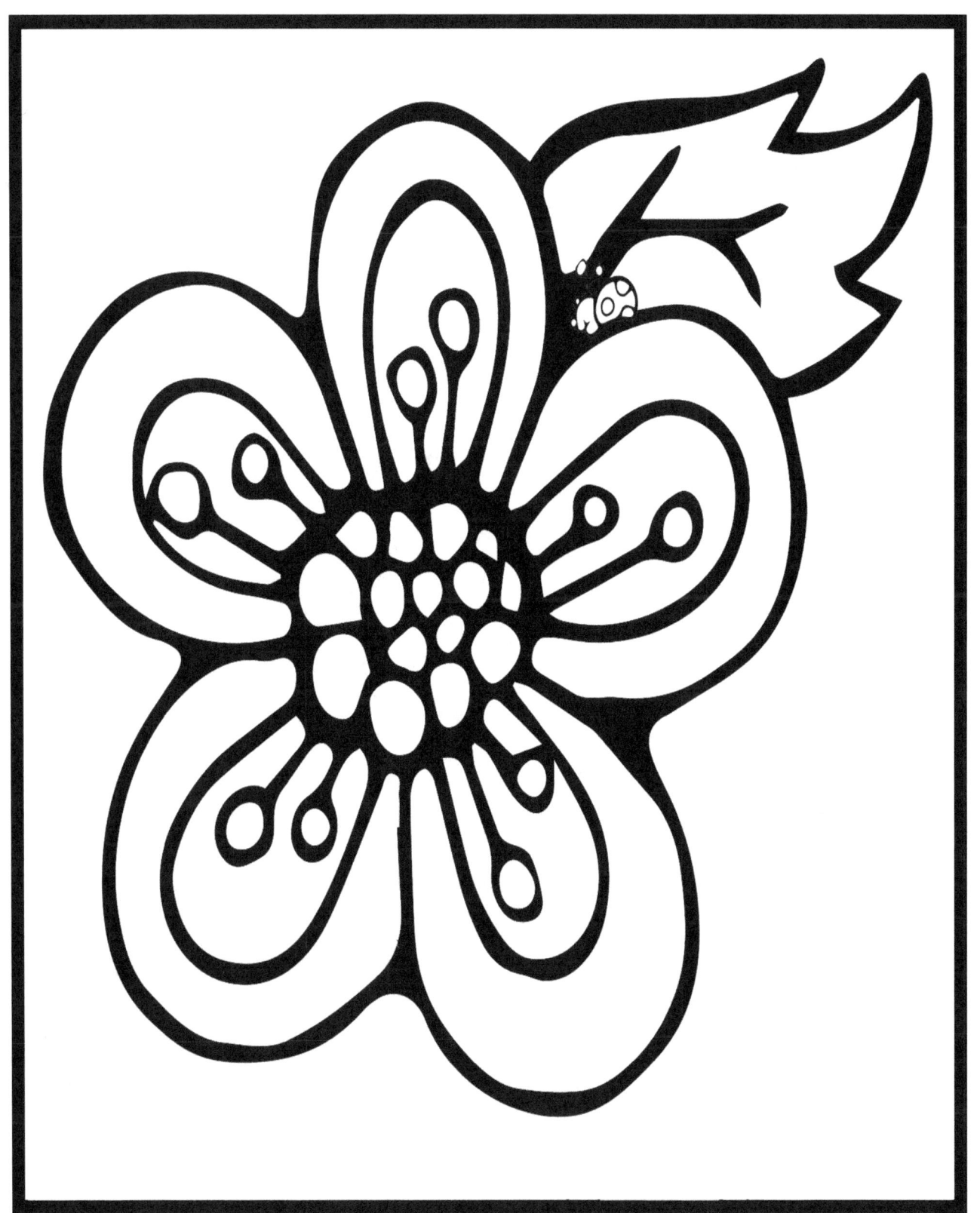

Bonnie S. MacLachlan

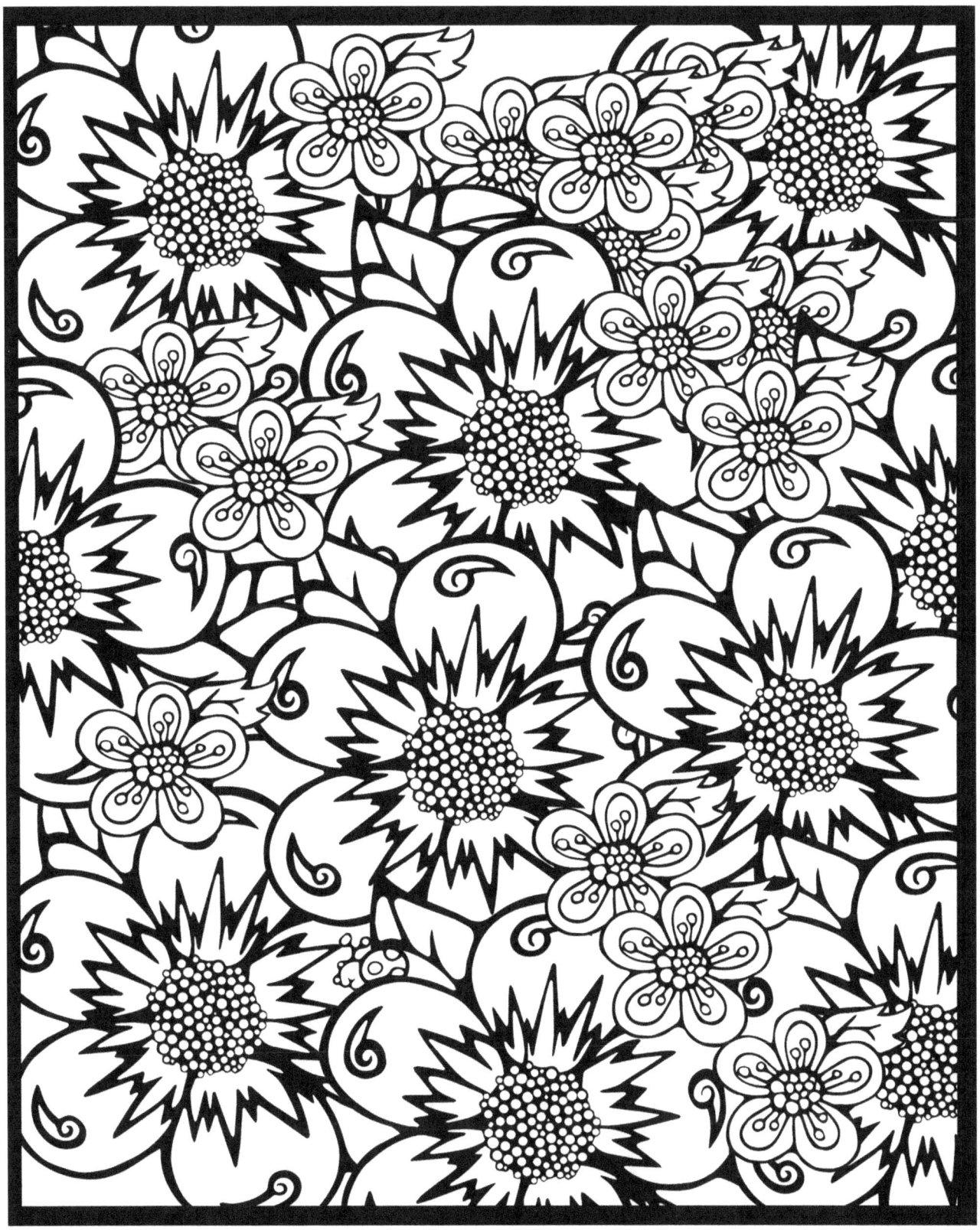

Bonnie S. MacLachlan

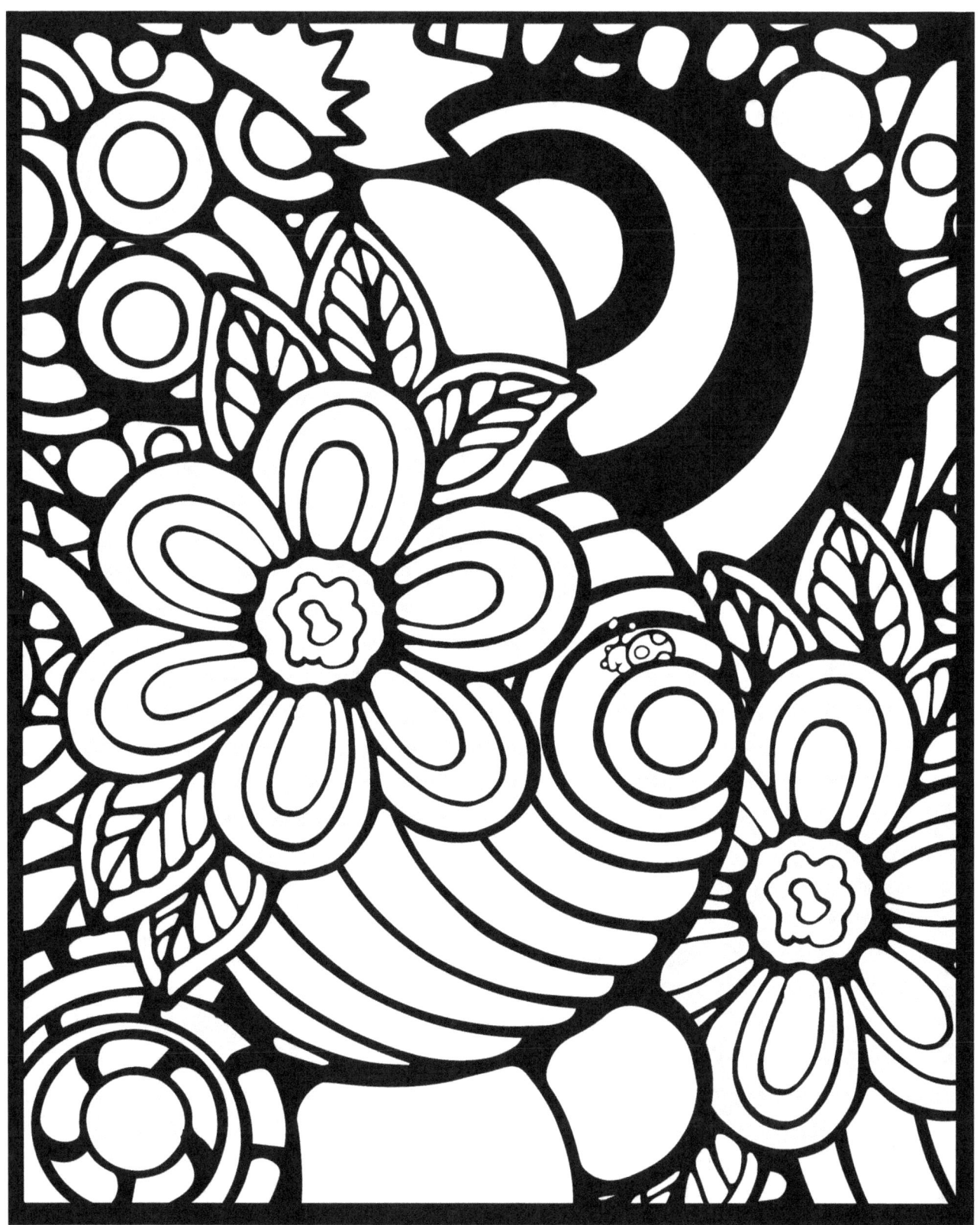

Bonnie S. MacLachlan

Color Me HaPpY

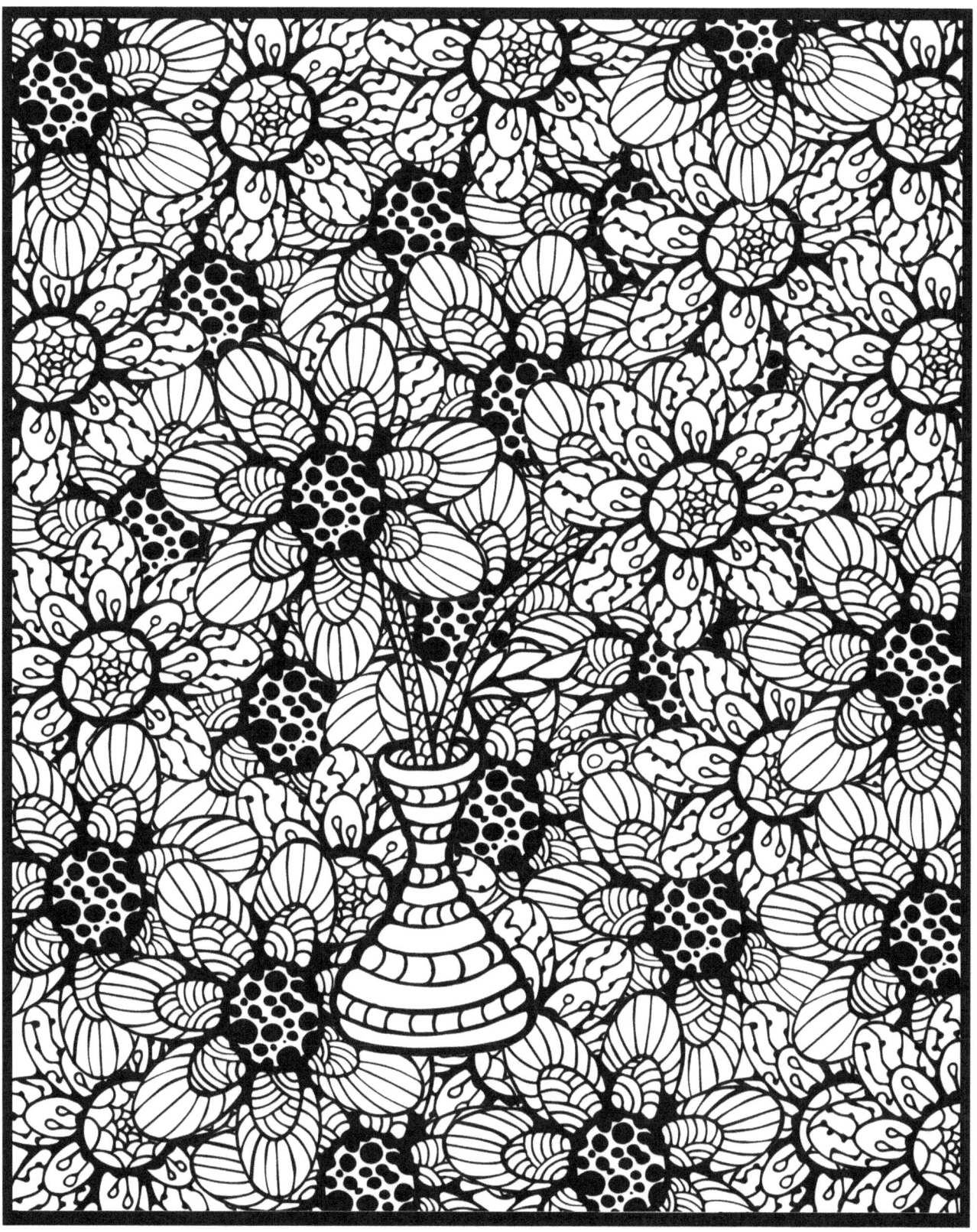

Bonnie S. MacLachlan

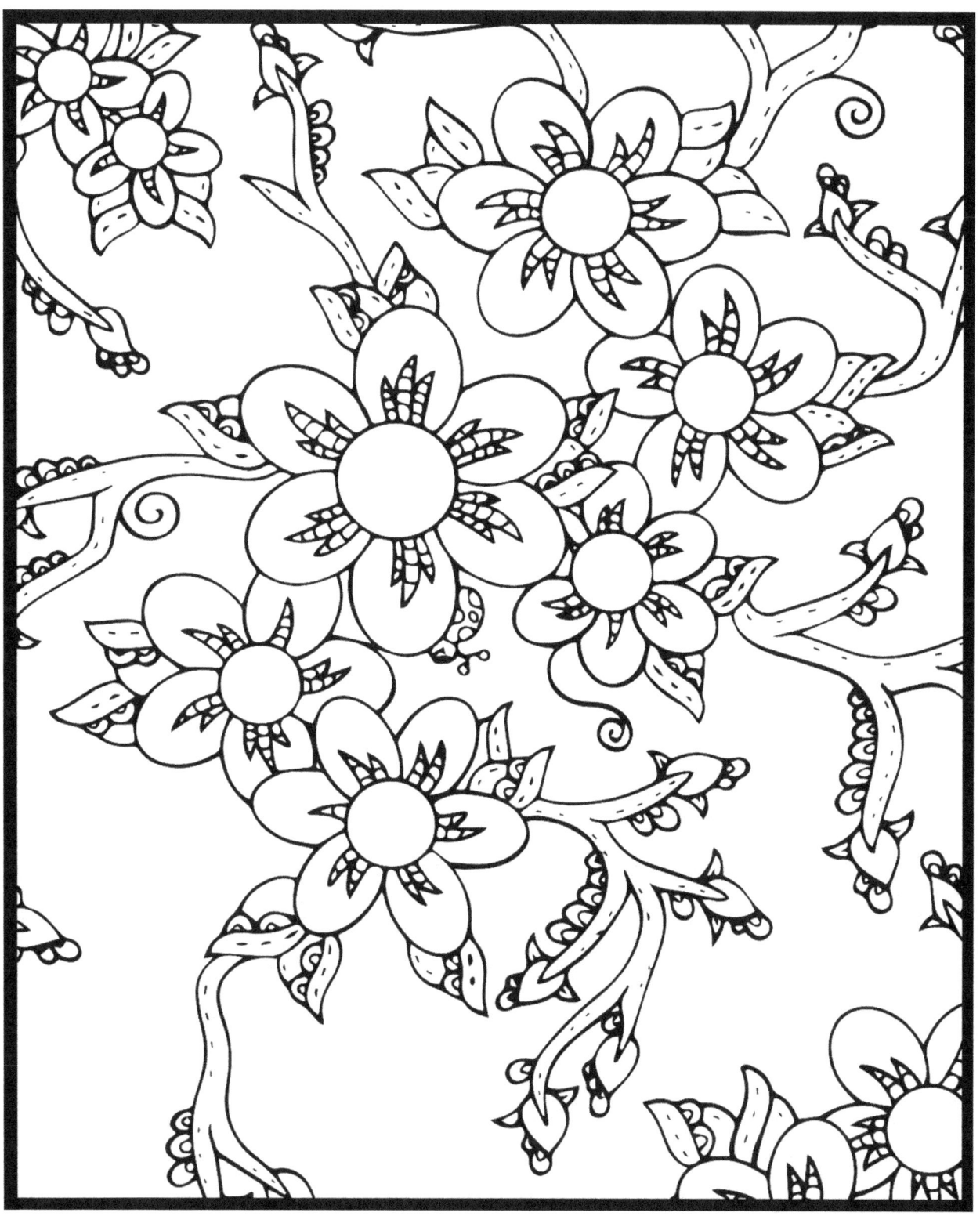

Bonnie S. MacLachlan

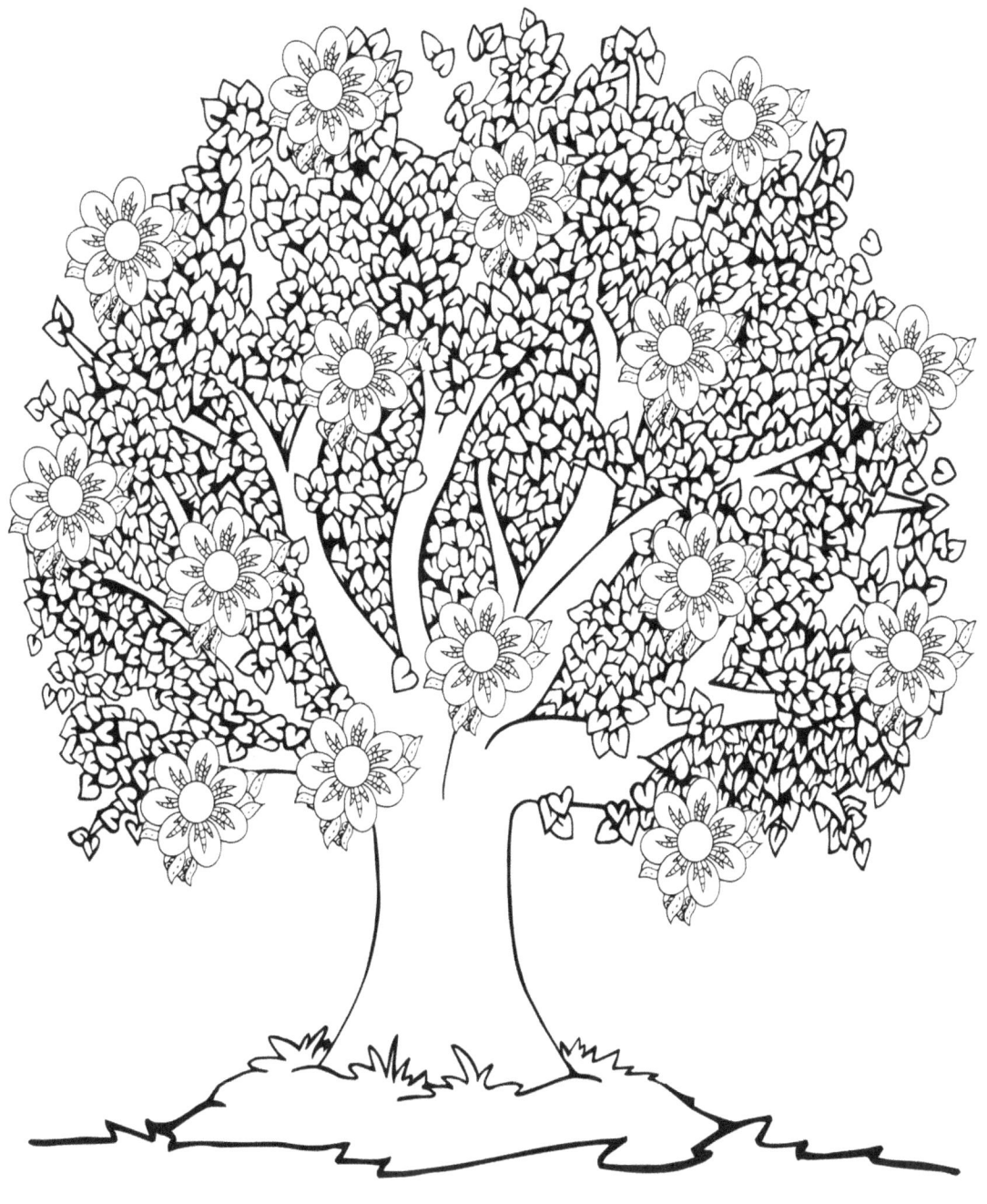

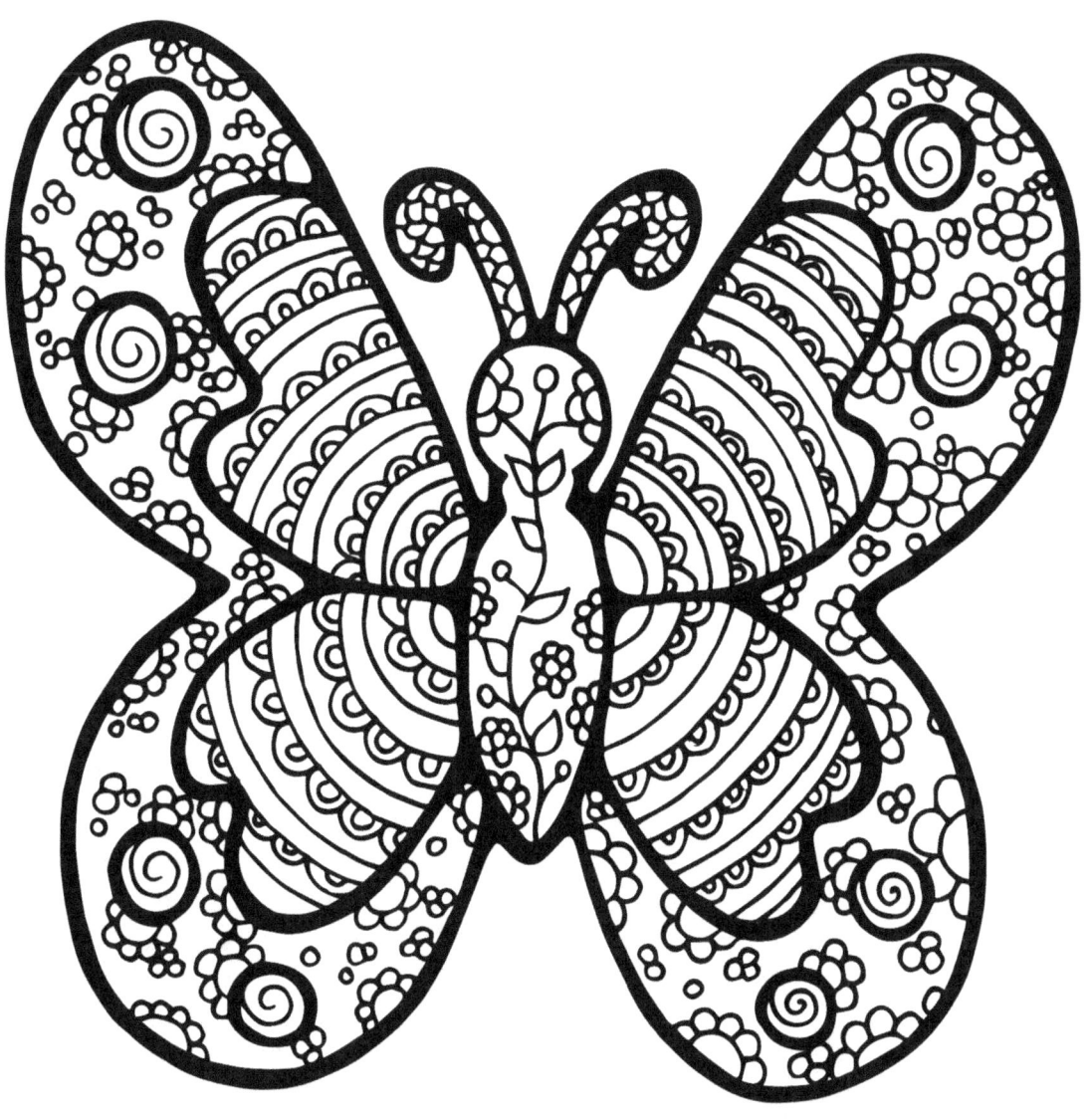

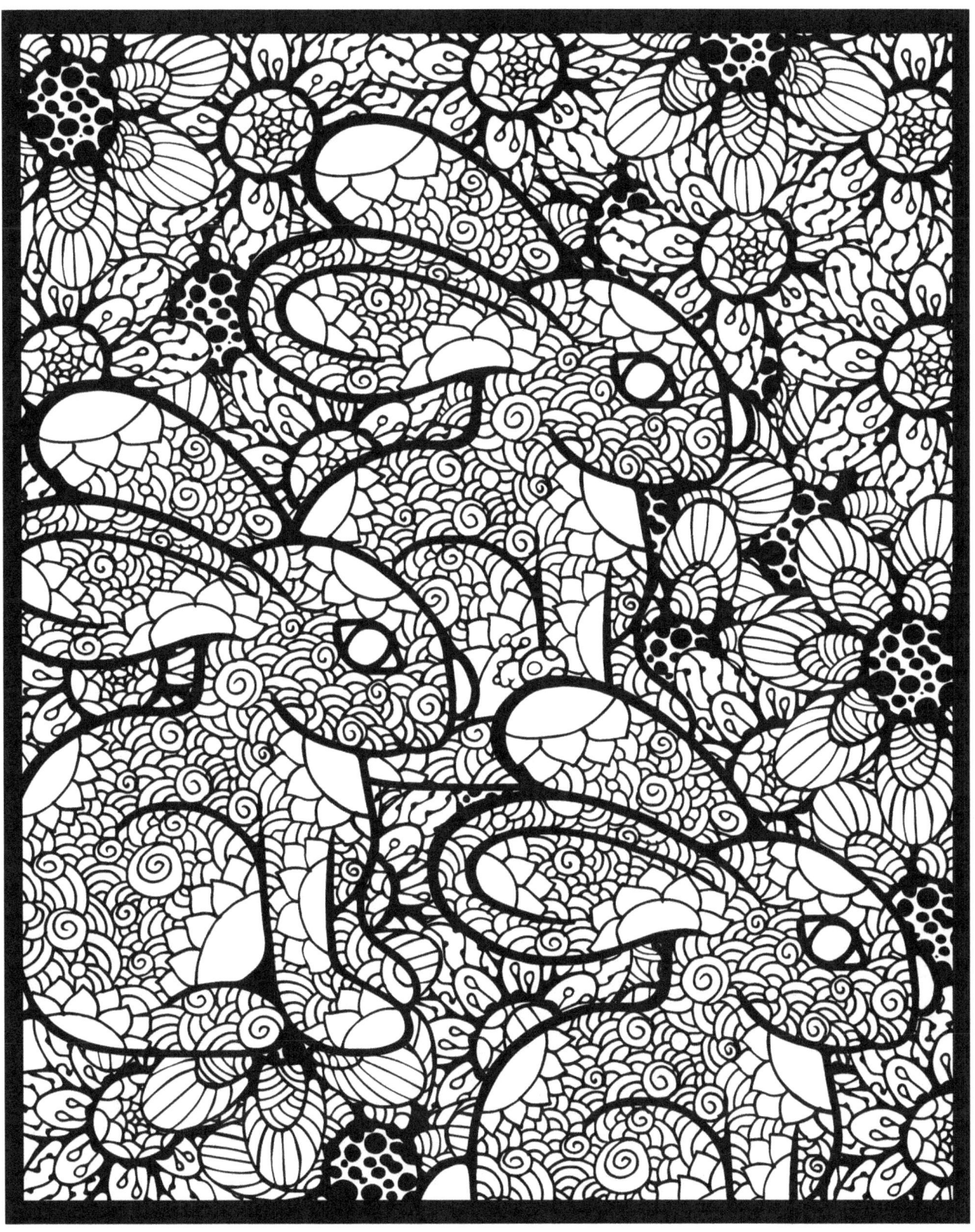

Bonnie S. MacLachlan

Color Me HaPpY

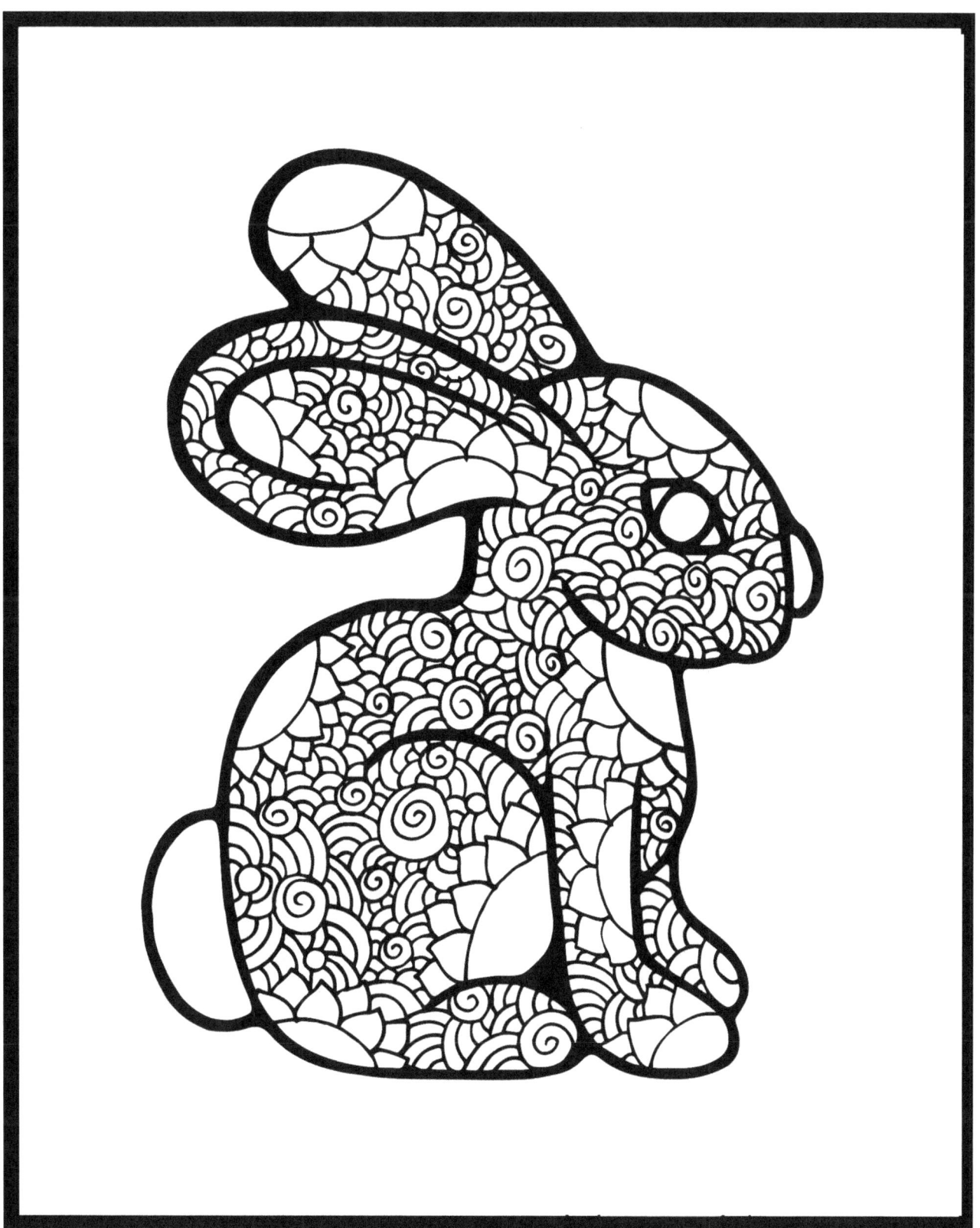

Bonnie S. MacLachlan

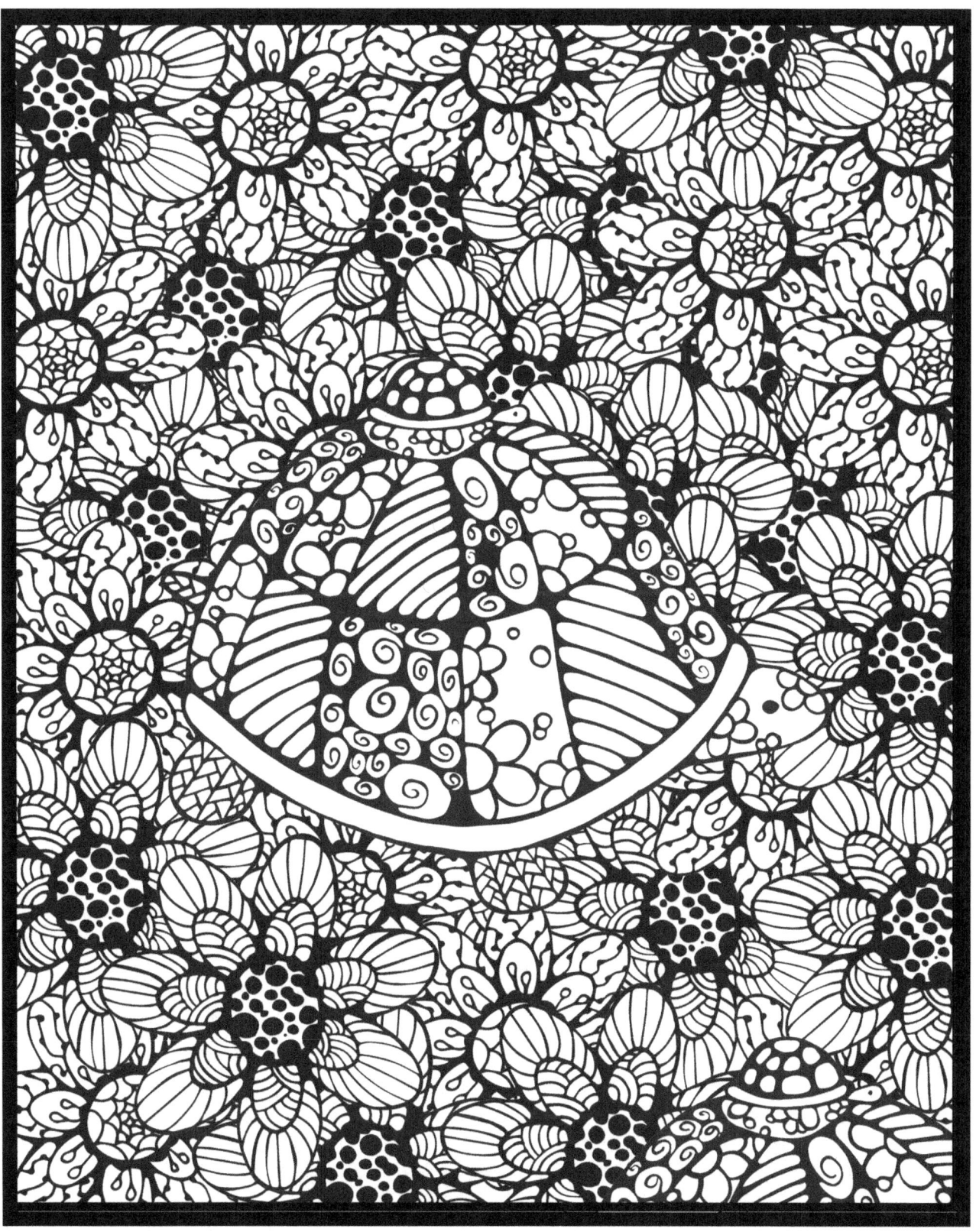

Bonnie S. MacLachlan

Color Me HaPpY

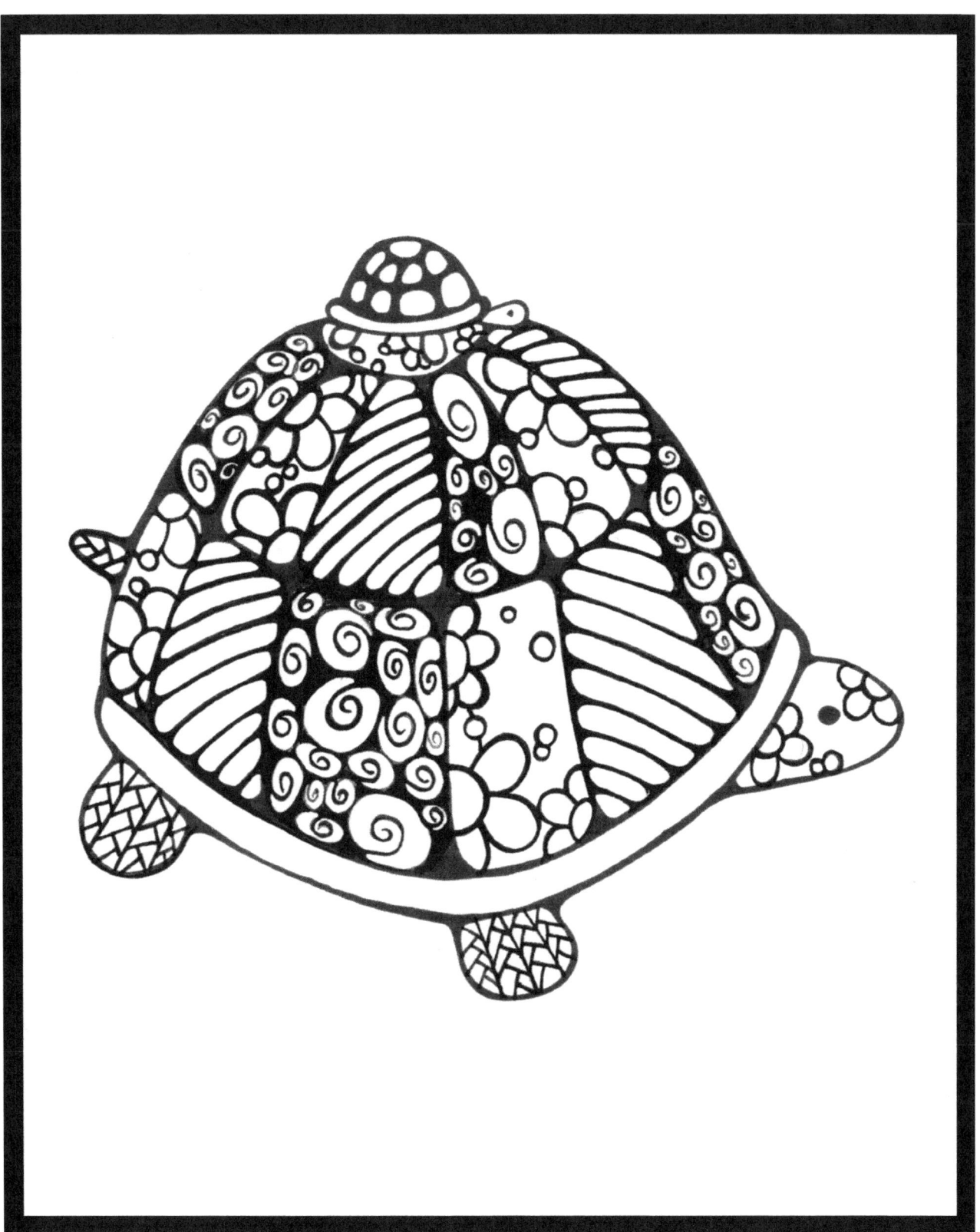

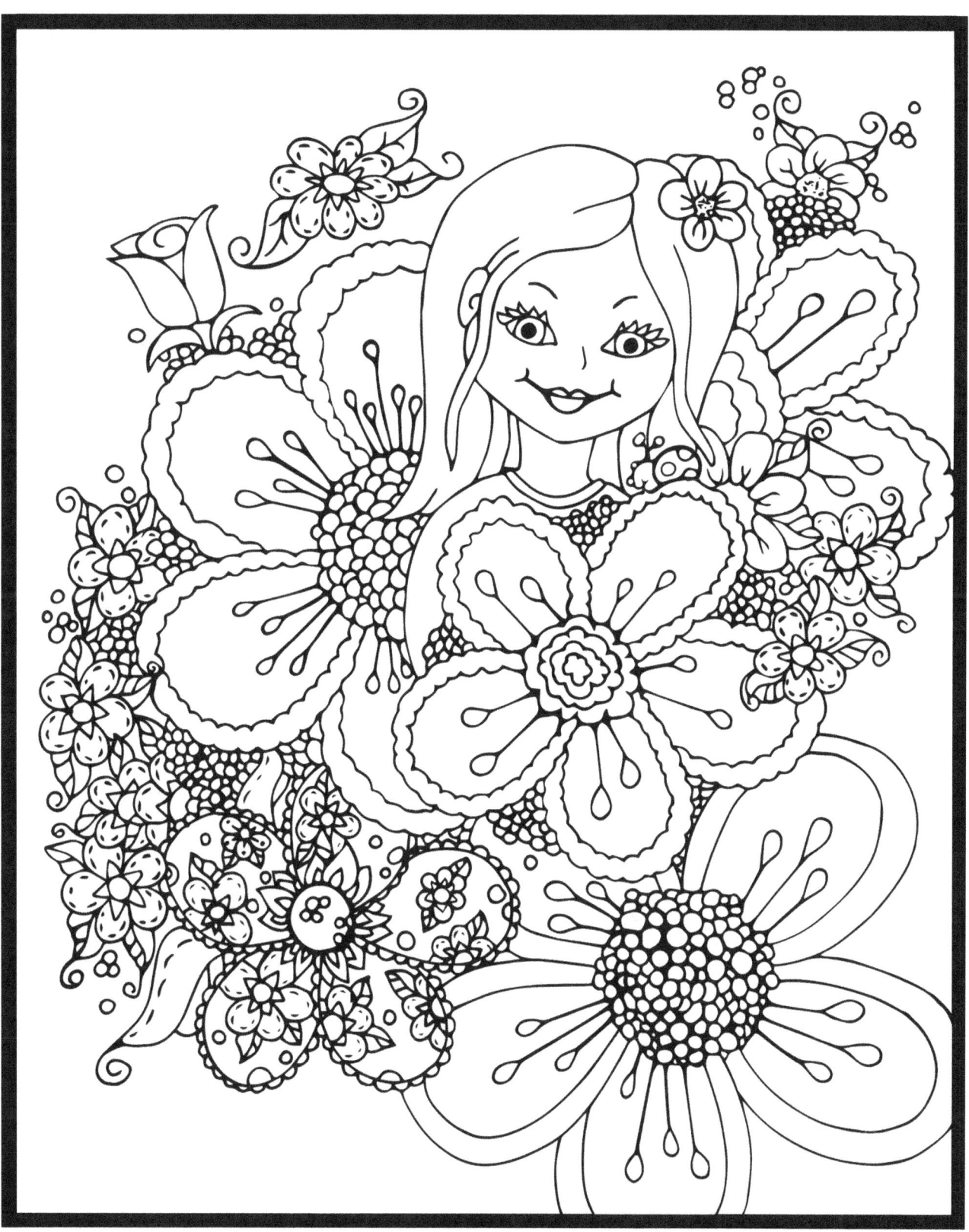

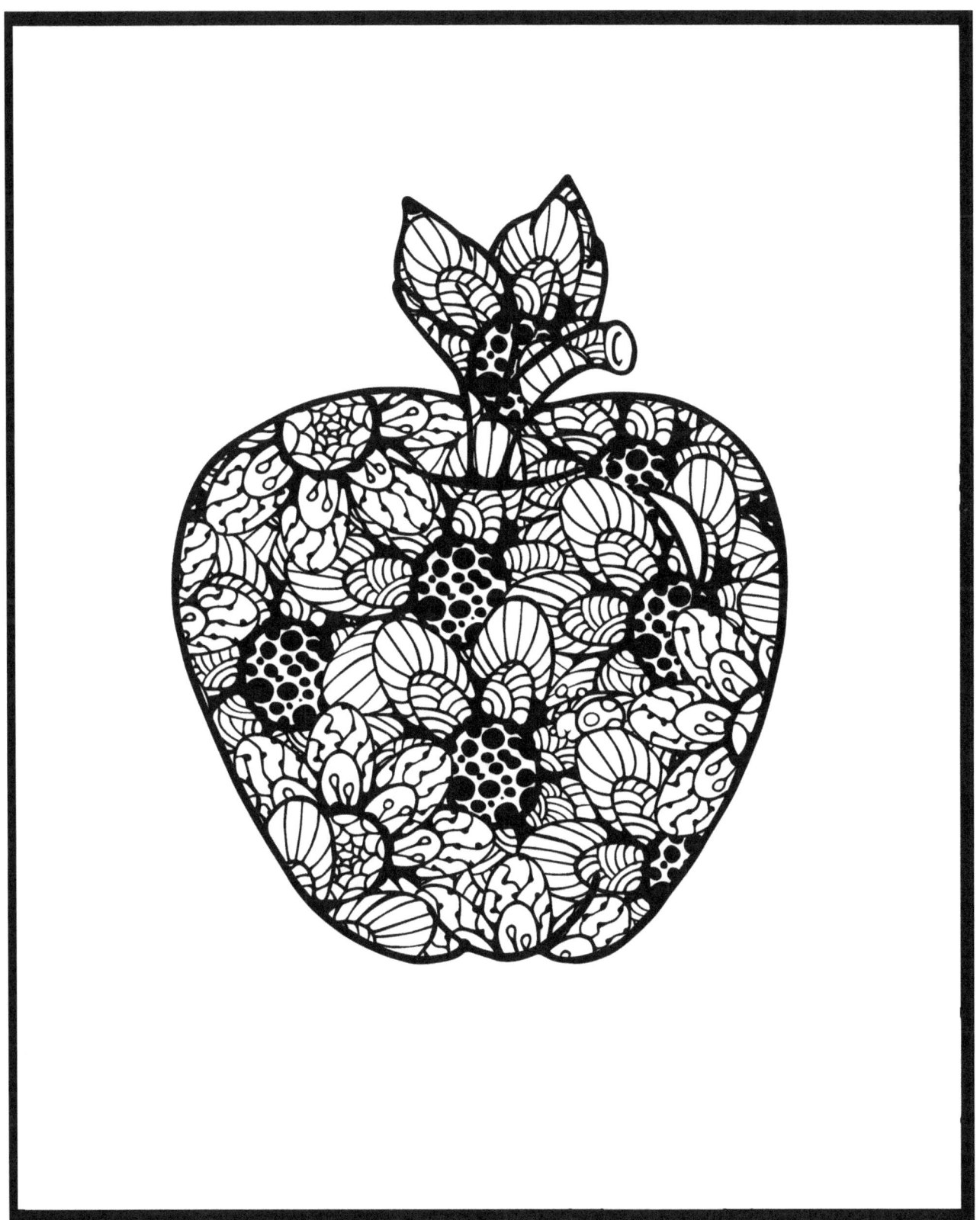

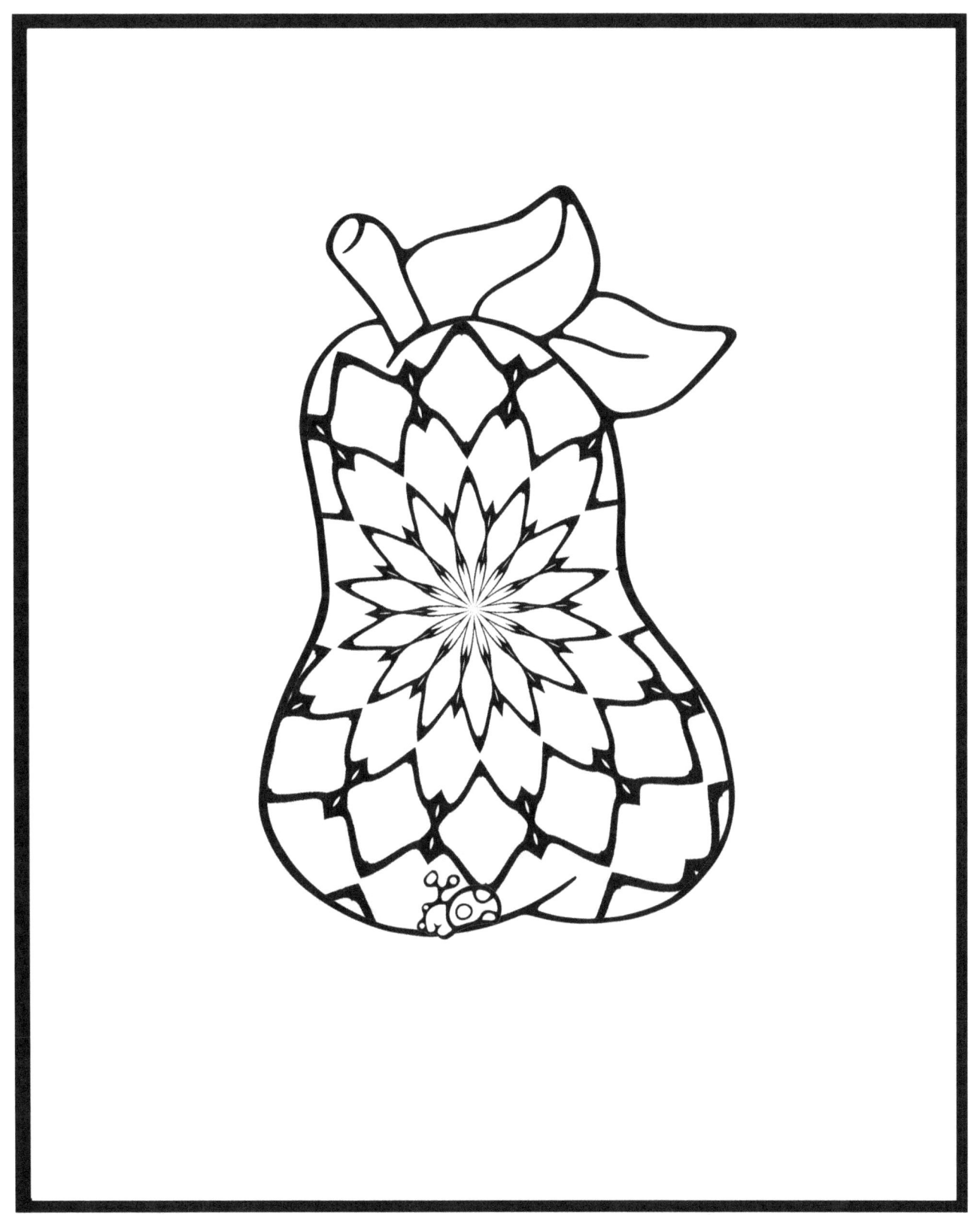

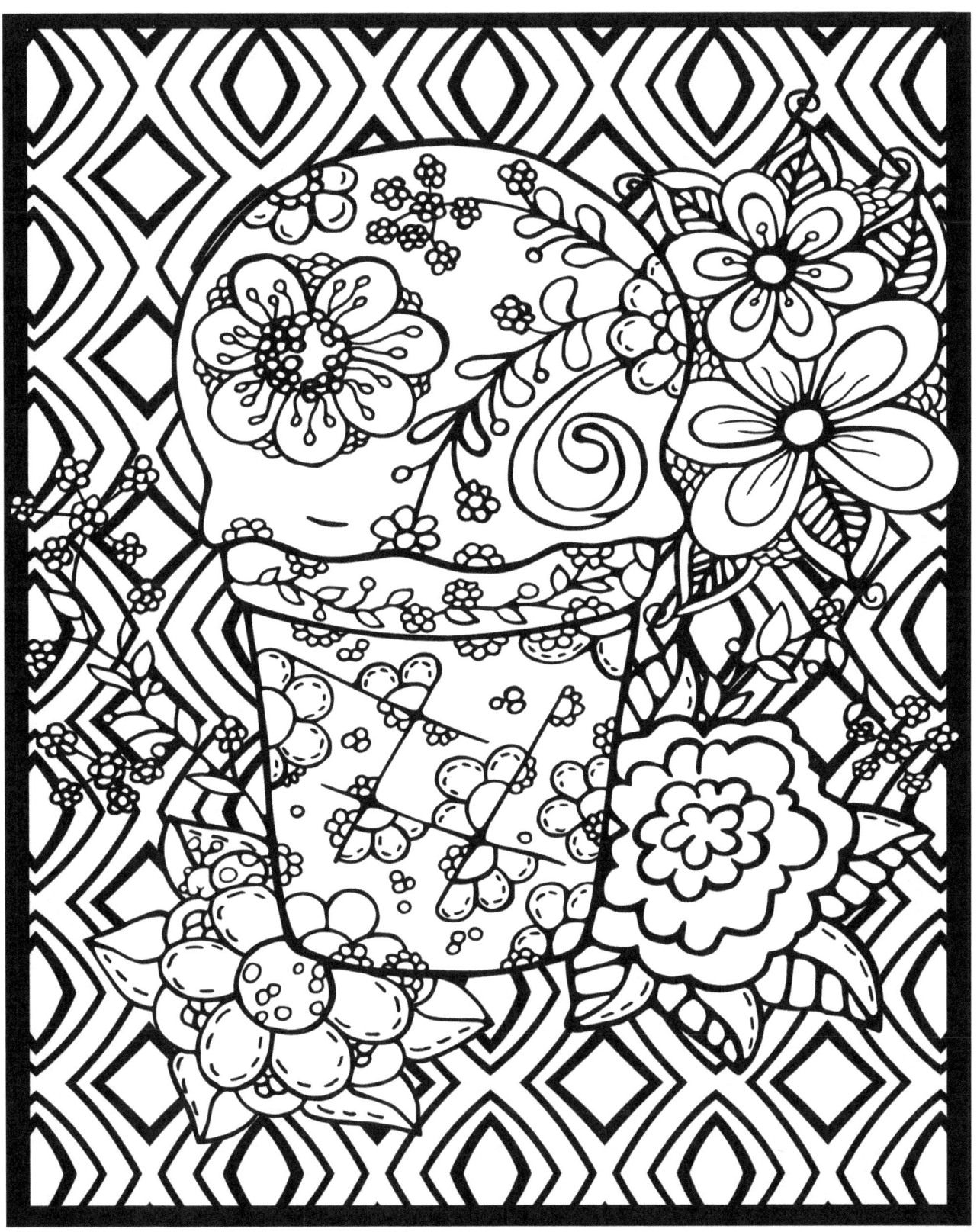

Bonnie S. MacLachlan

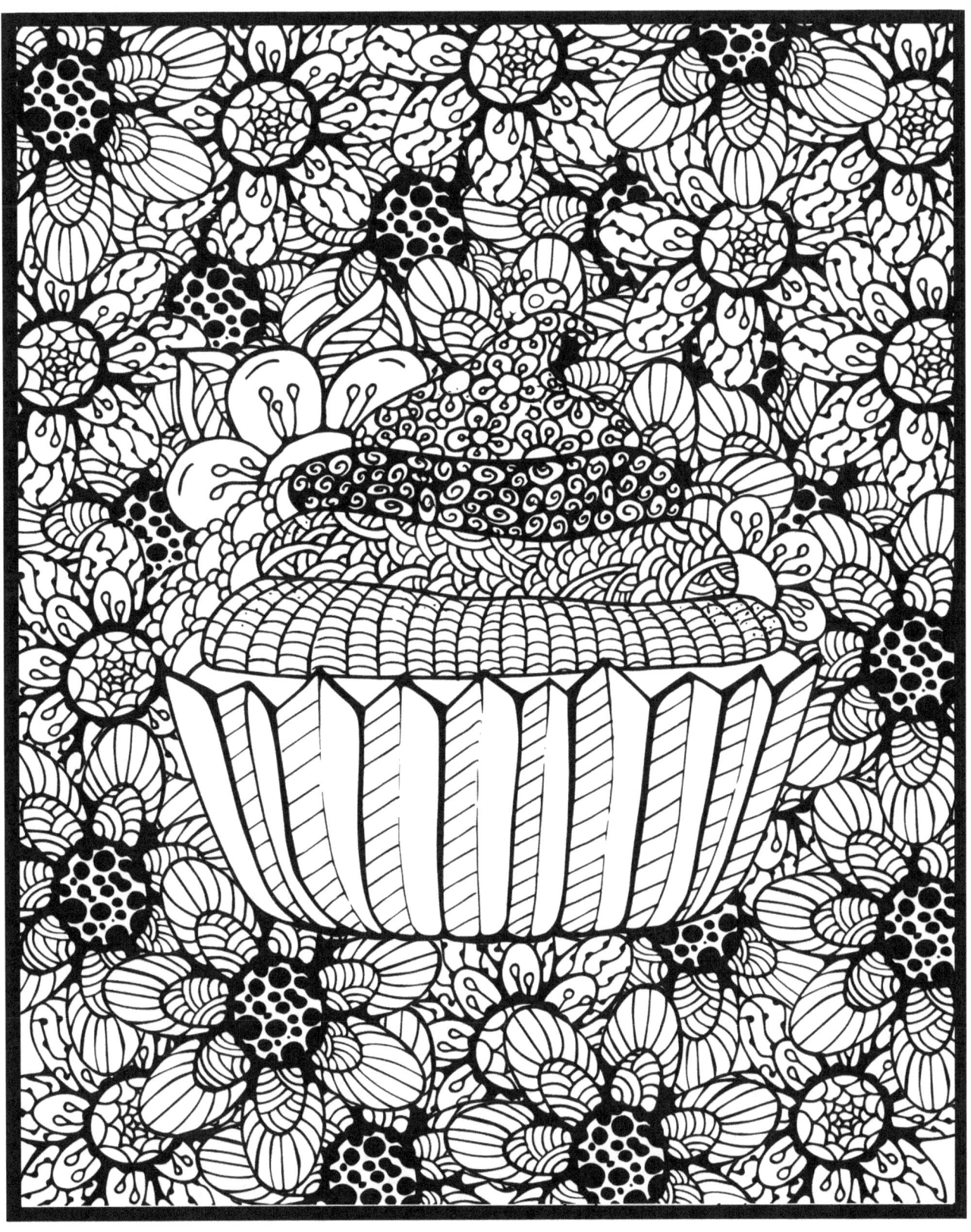

Bonnie S. MacLachlan

Bonnie S. MacLachlan

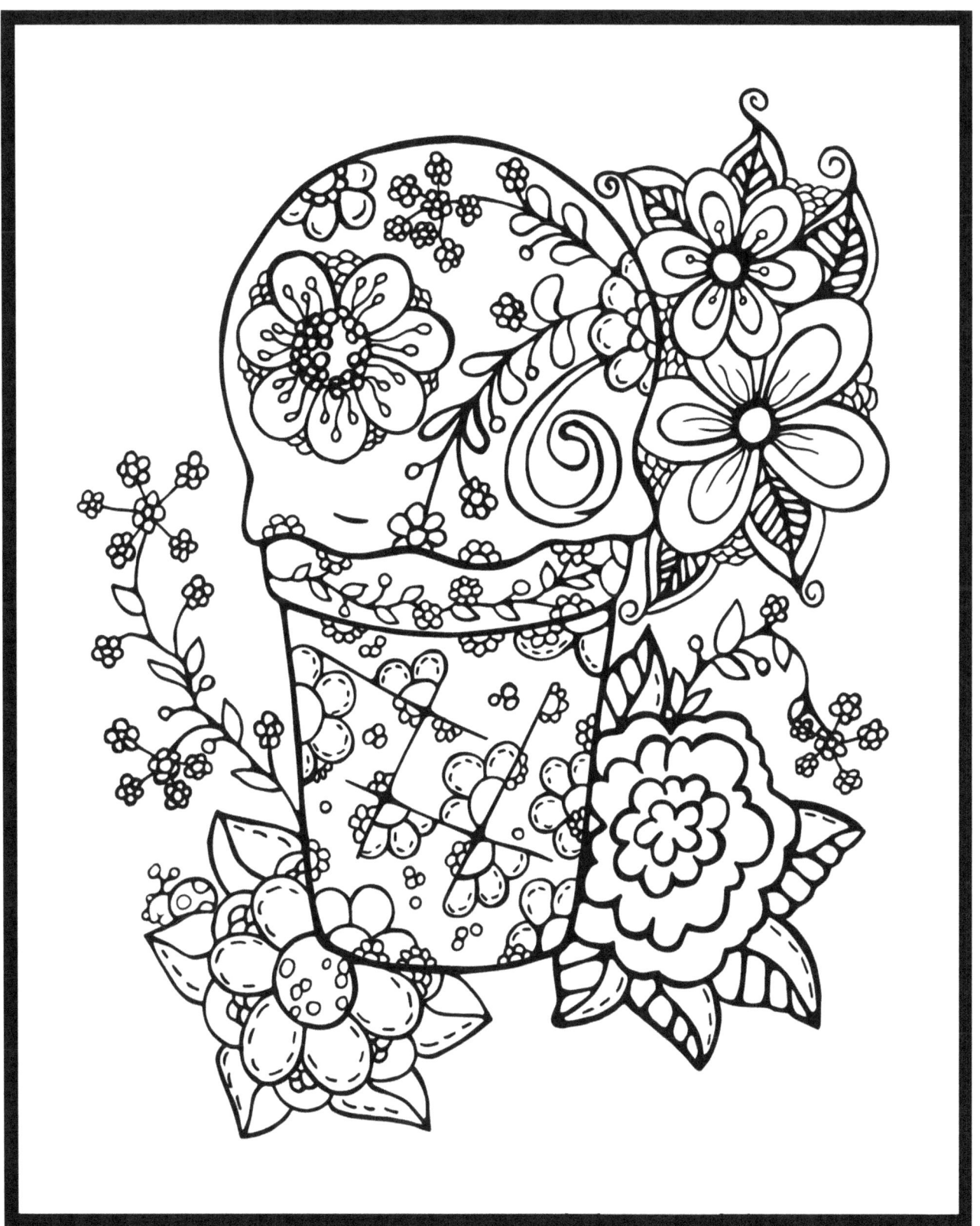

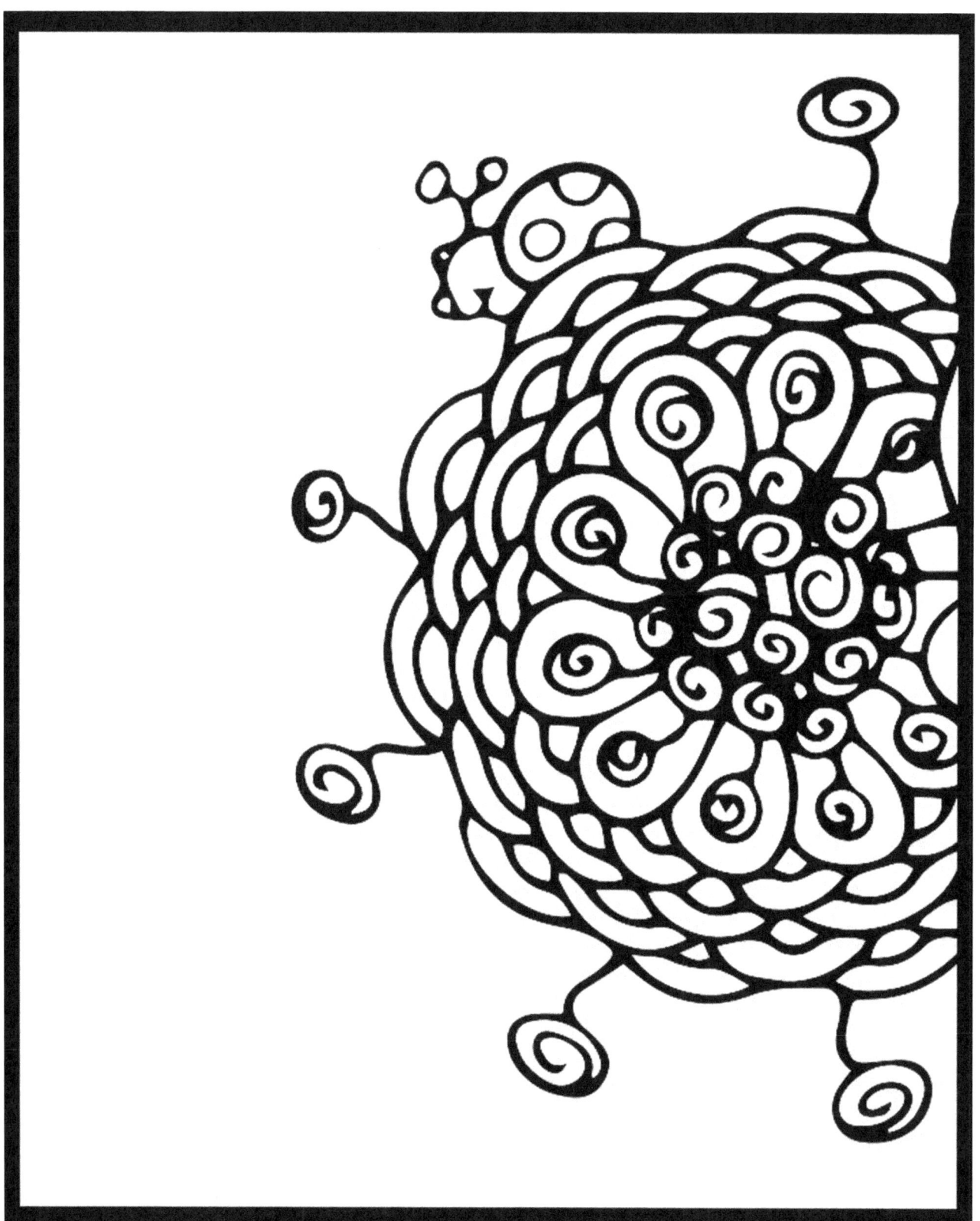

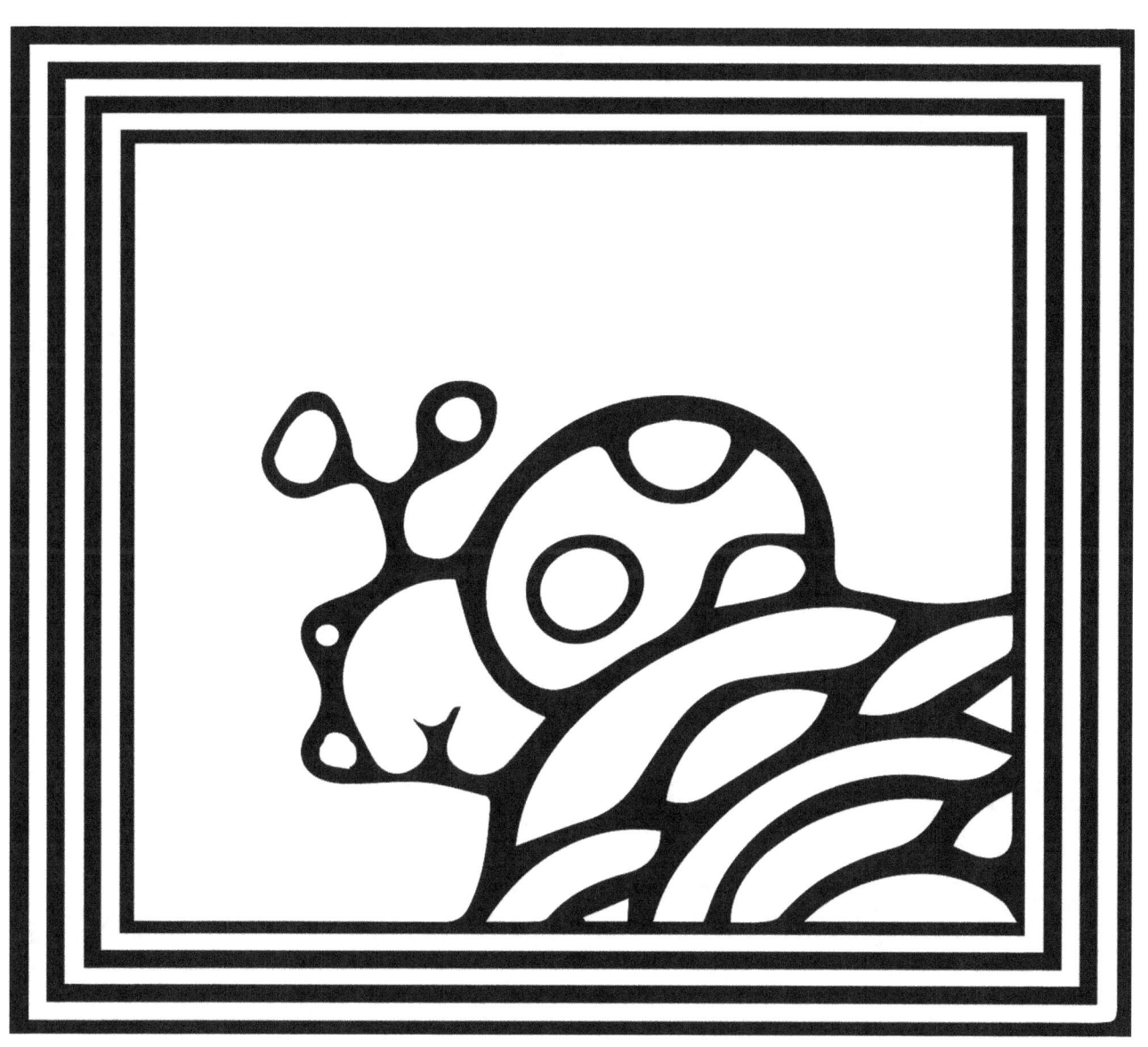

Bonnie S. MacLachlan

Color Me HaPpY

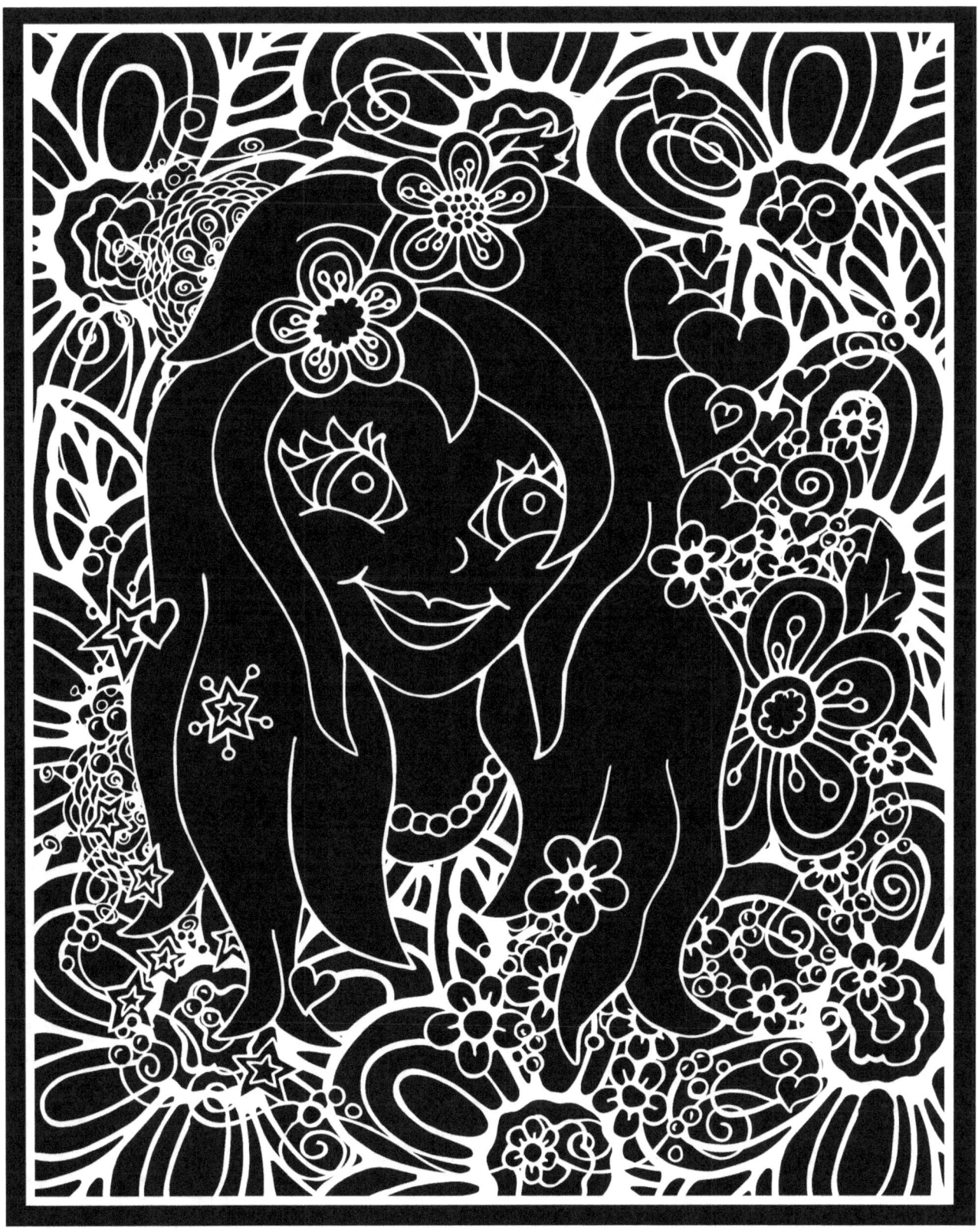

Bonnie S. MacLachlan

Color Me HaPpY

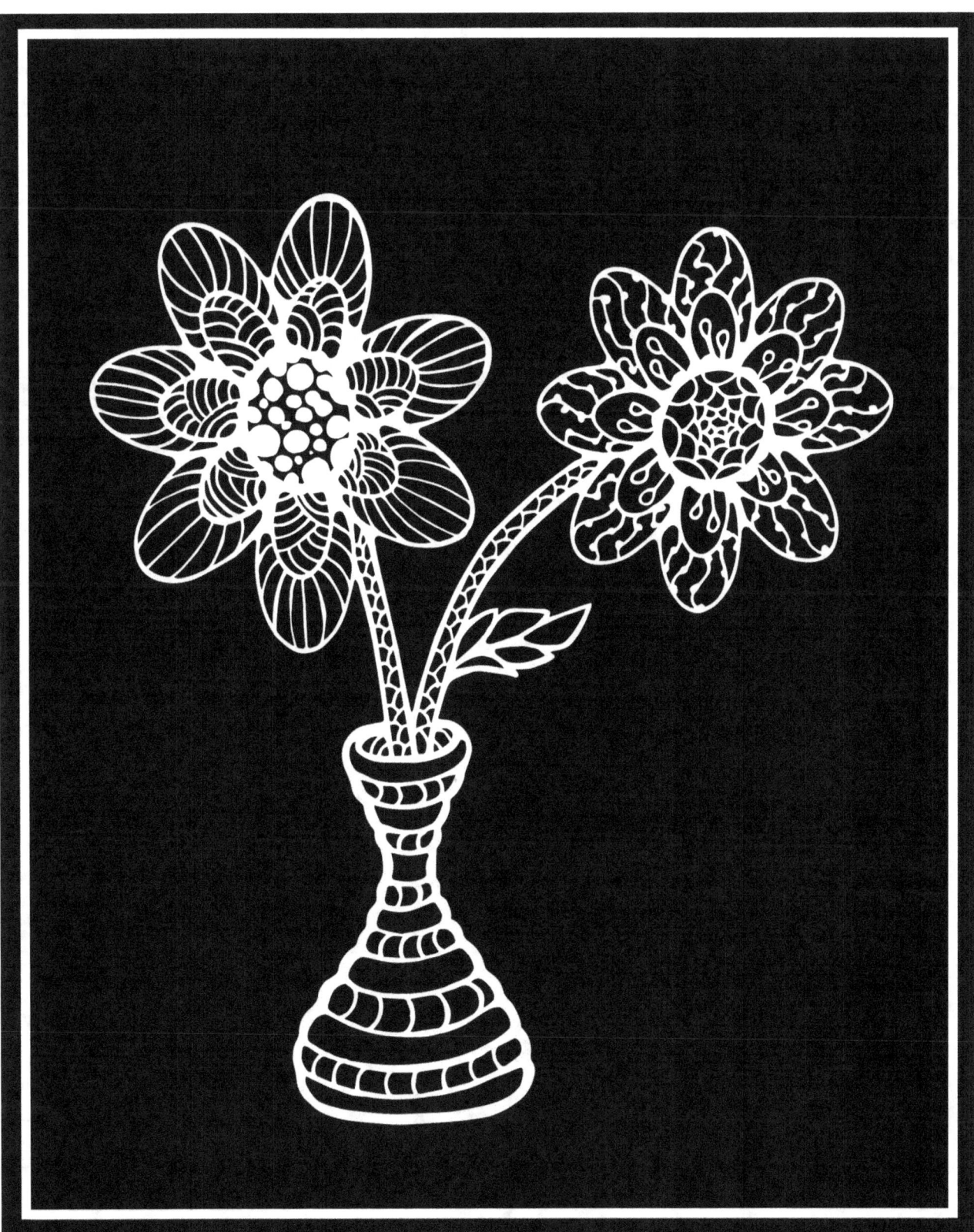

Bonnie S. MacLachlan

Bonnie S. MacLachlan

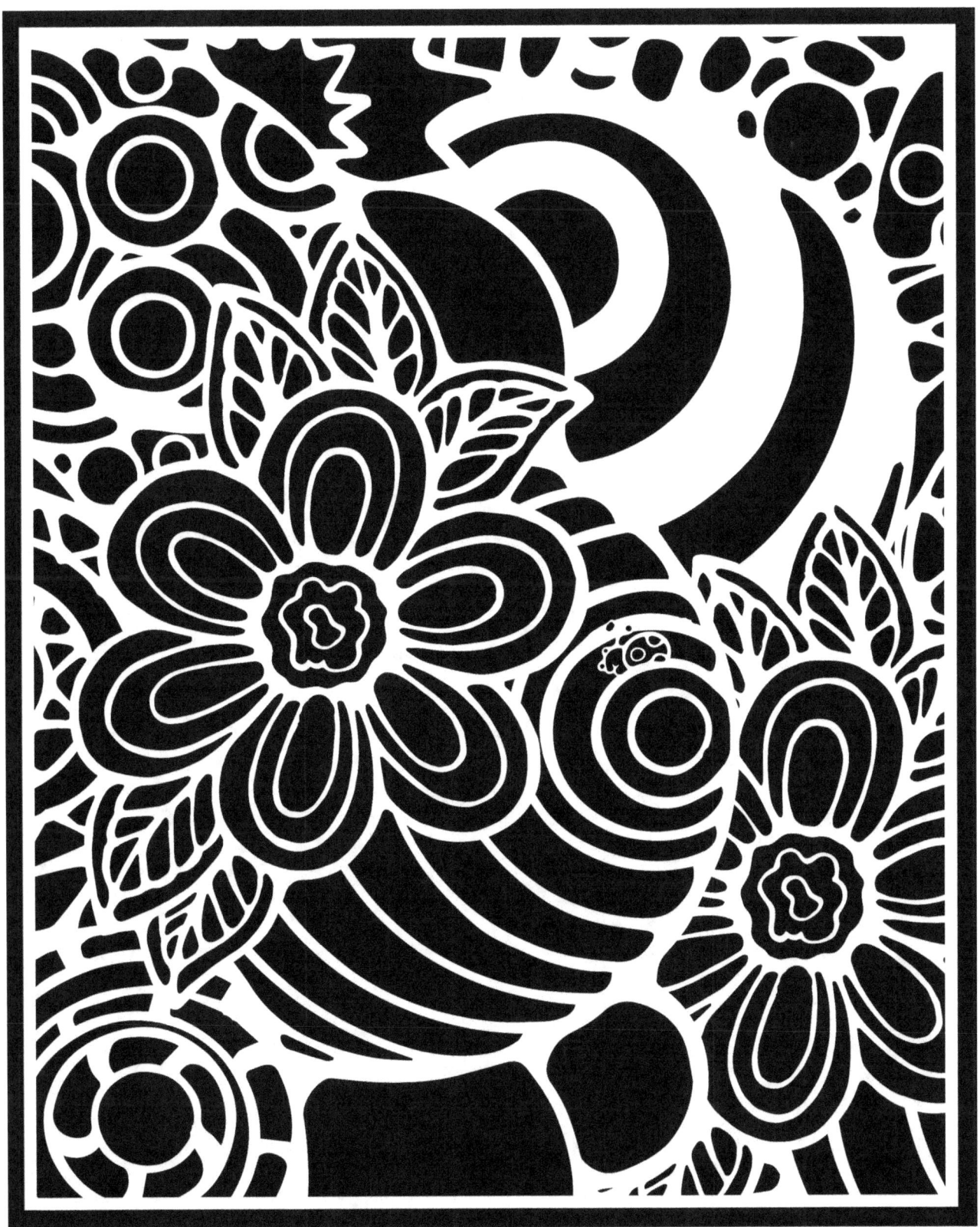

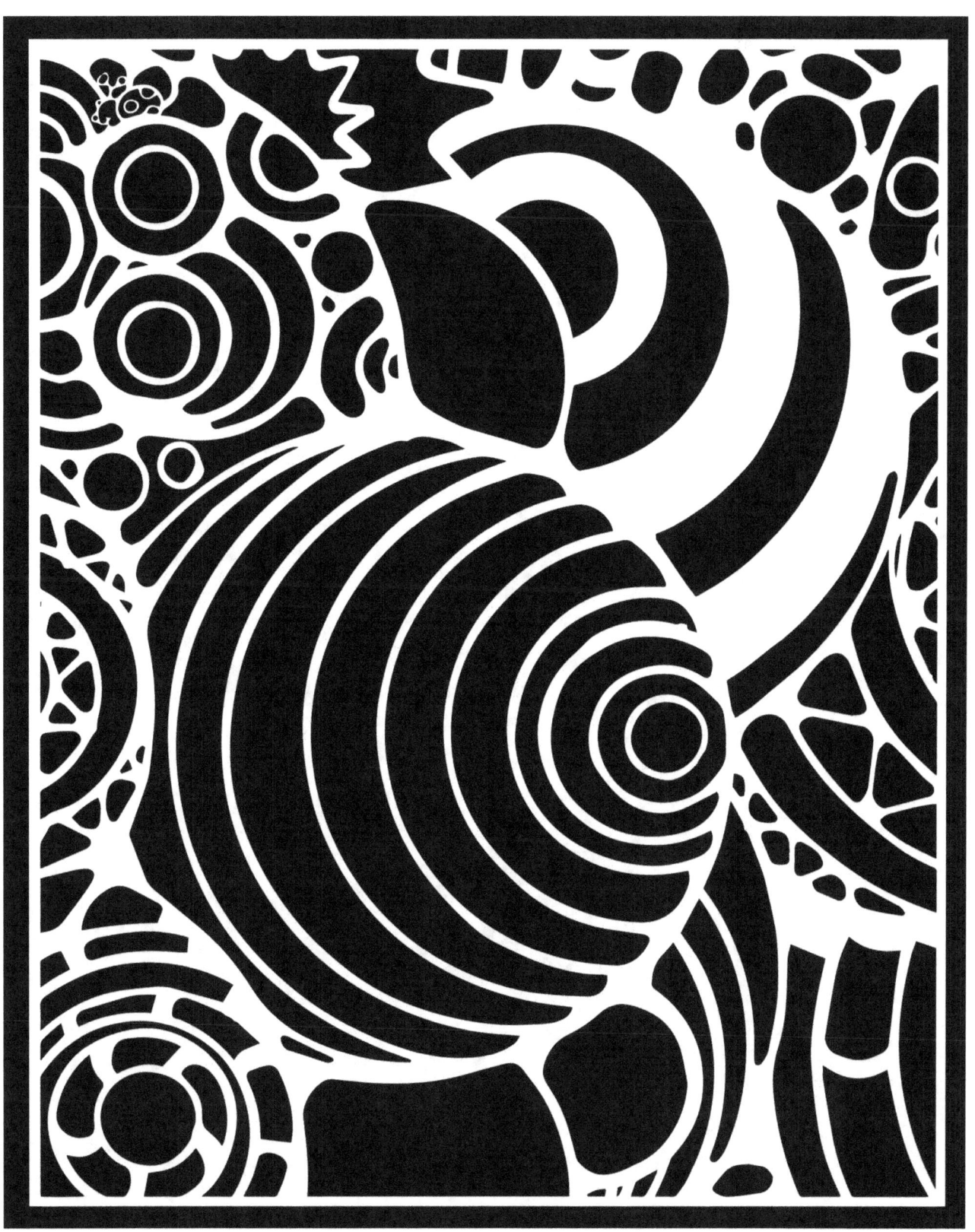

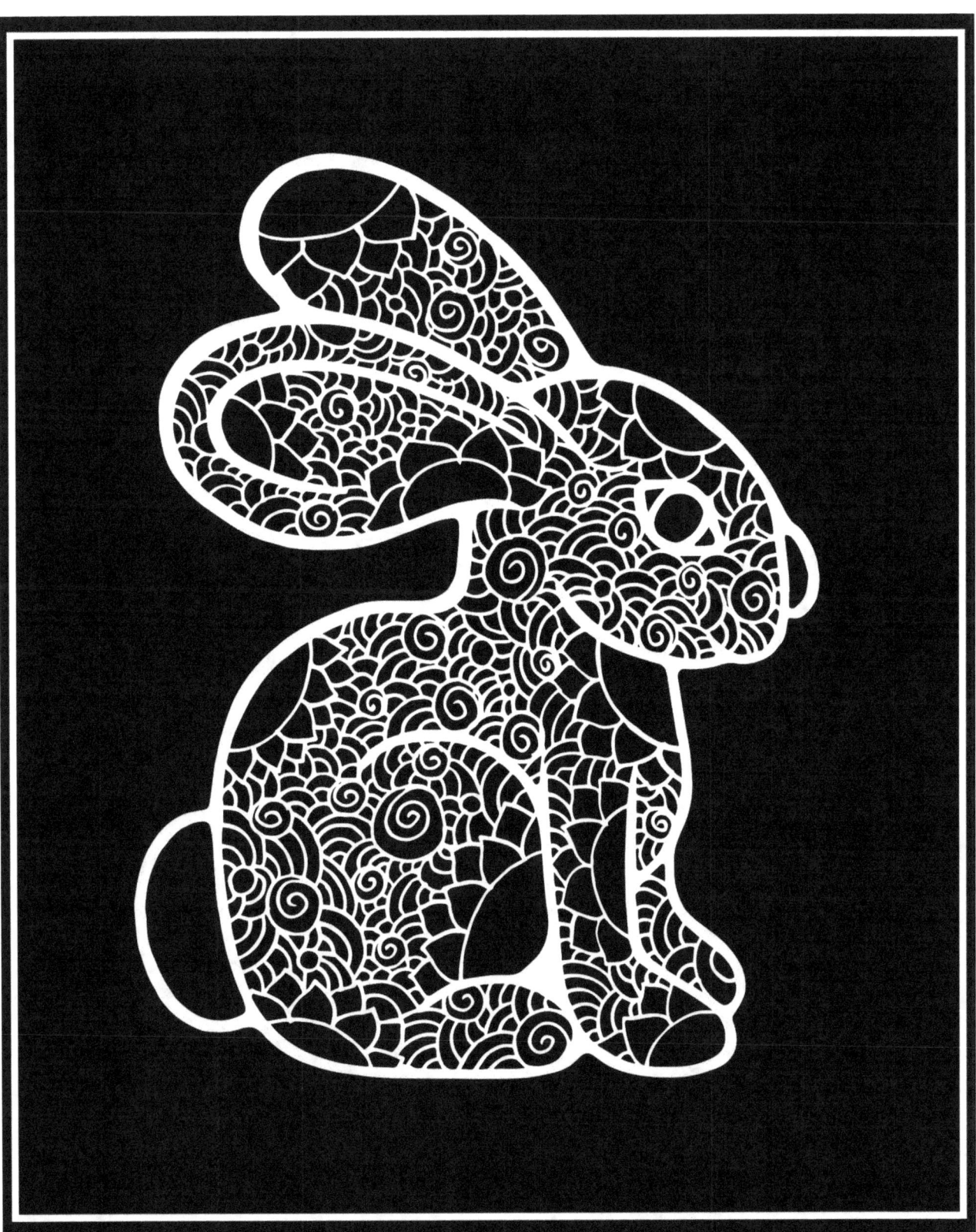

Bonnie S. MacLachlan

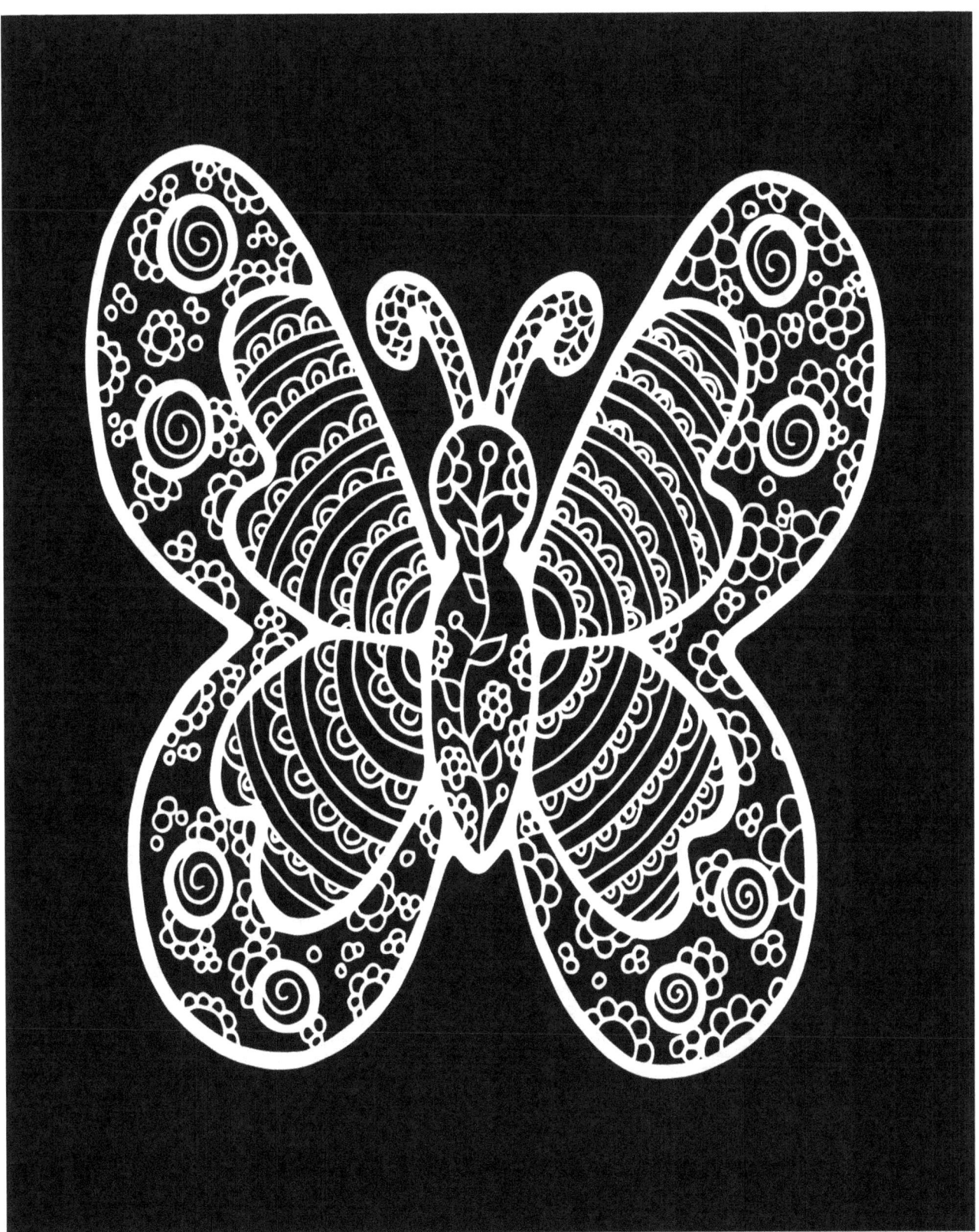

Bonnie S. MacLachlan

Color Me HaPpY

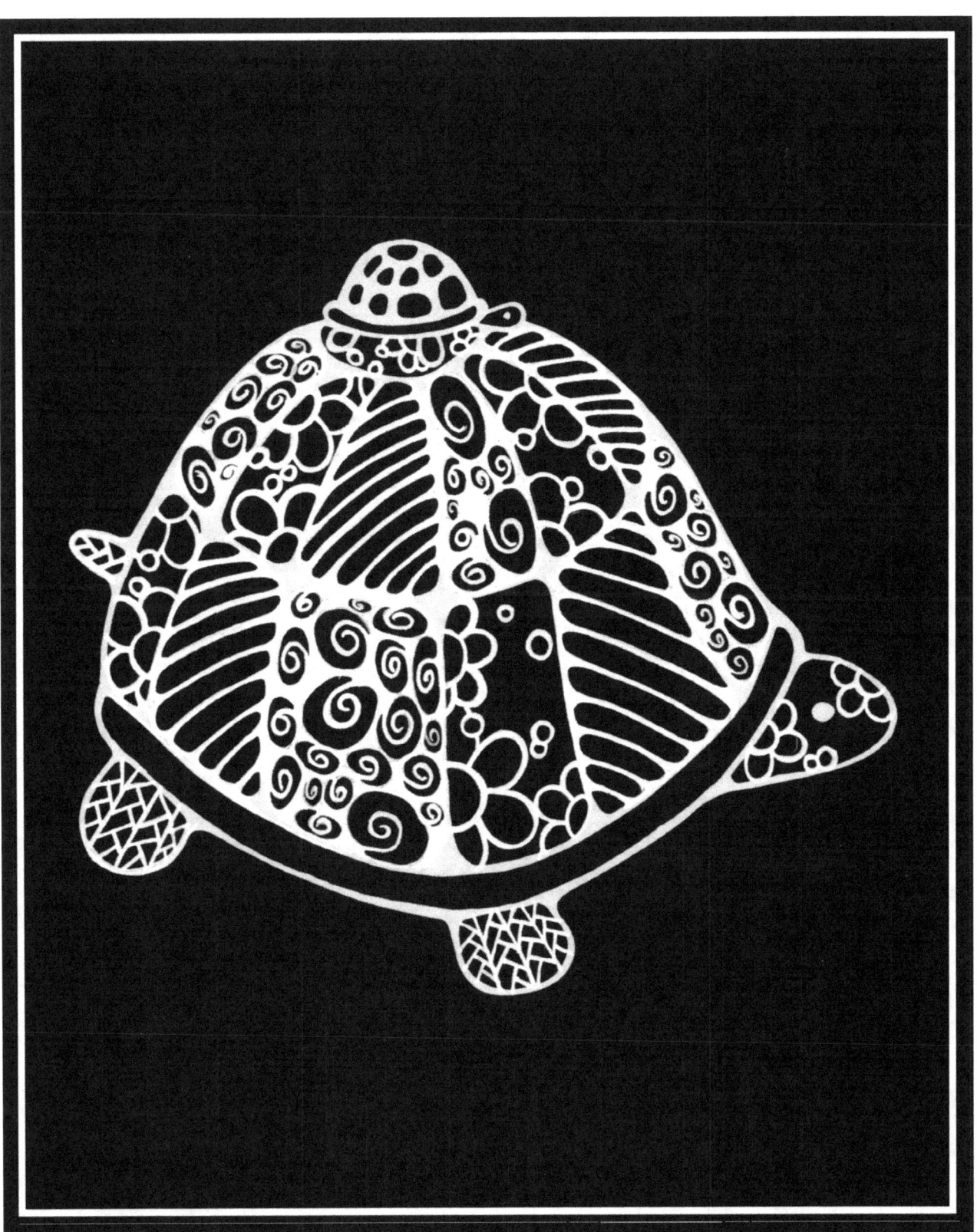

Bonnie S. MacLachlan

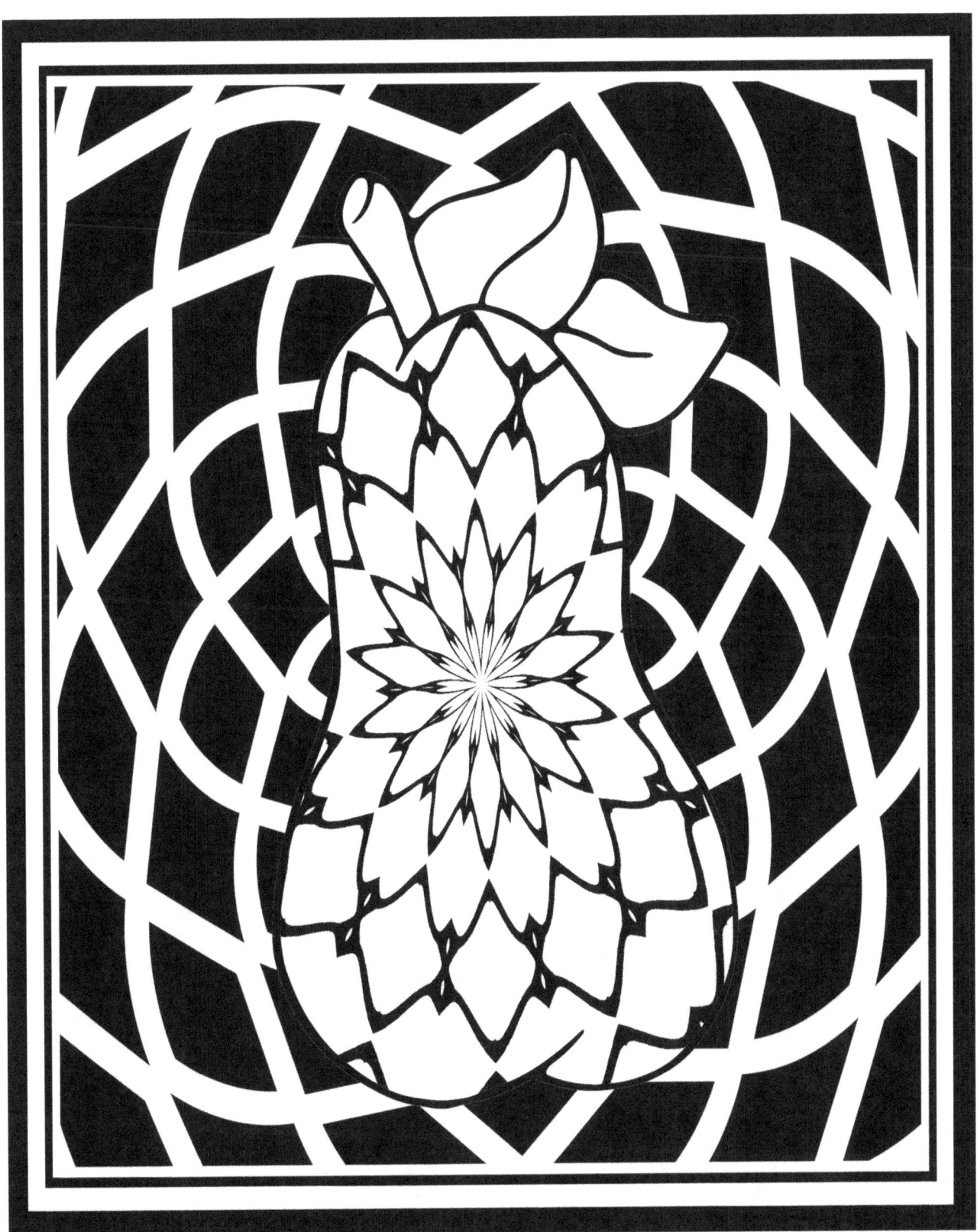

Bonnie S. MacLachlan

Color Me HaPpY

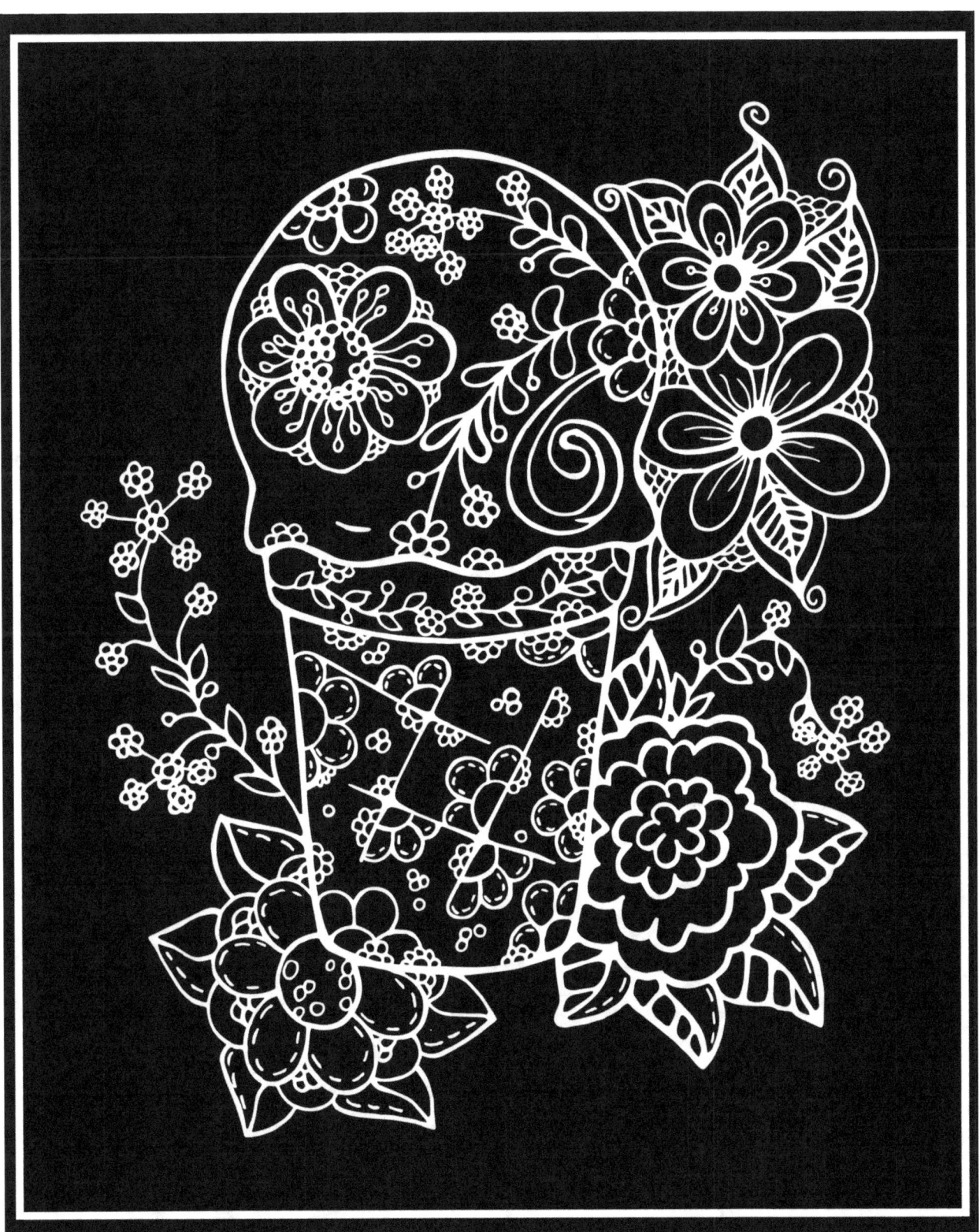

Bonnie S. MacLachlan

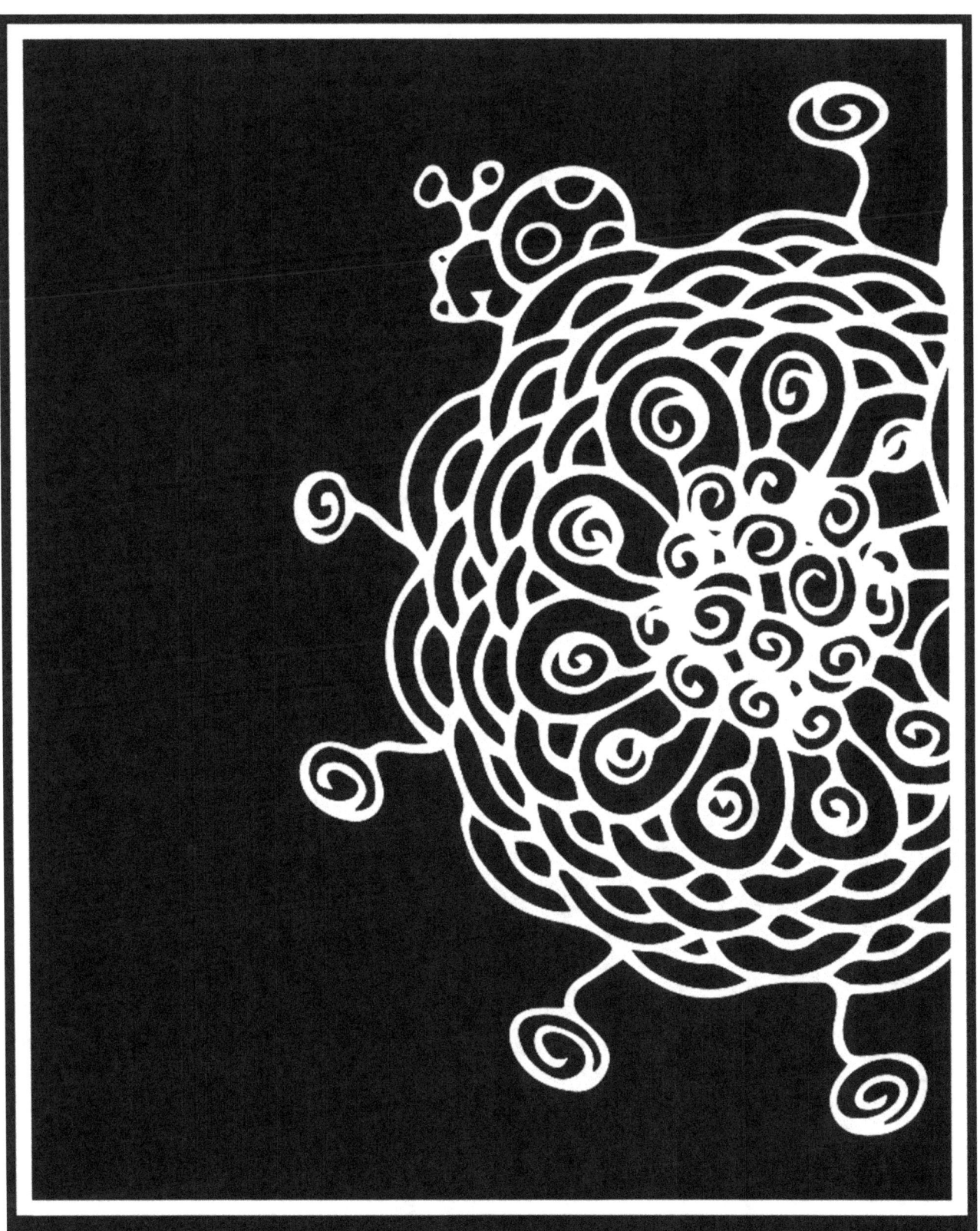

Bonnie S. MacLachlan

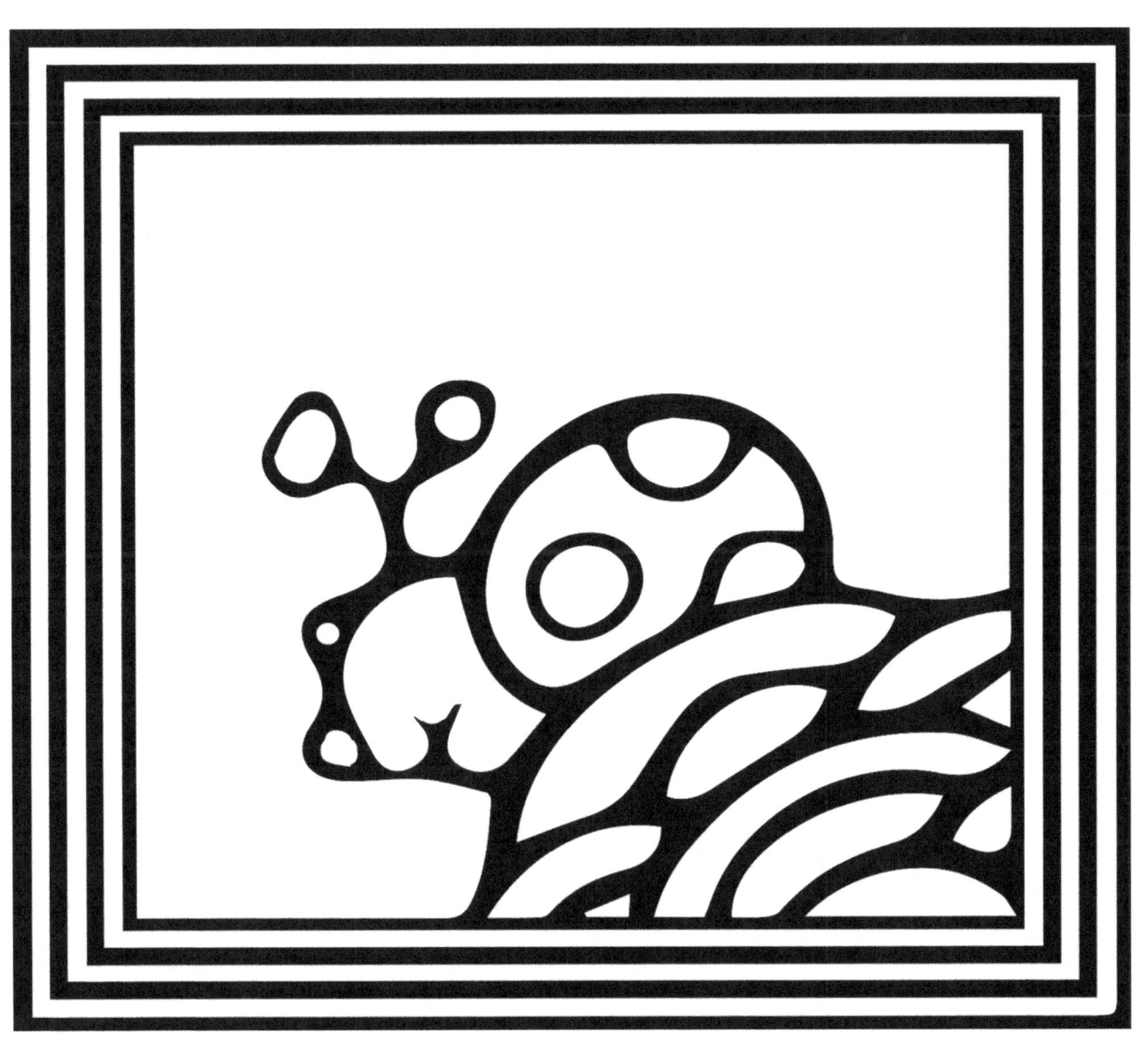

See You In Our Next Coloring Adventure ....